OXFORD INTENSIVE ENGLISH COUR.

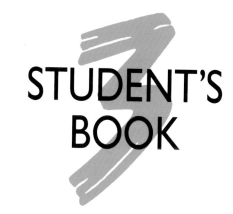

STUDENT'S
BOOK

DAVID BOLTON
CLIVE OXENDEN
LEN PETERSON

Oxford University Press

Oxford University Press,
Walton Street, Oxford OX2 6DP

Oxford New York Toronto Madrid
Kuala Lumpur Singapore Hong Kong Tokyo
Delhi Bombay Madras Calcutta Karachi
Nairobi Dar es Salaam Cape Town
Melbourne Auckland

and associated companies in
Berlin Ibadan

OXFORD and OXFORD ENGLISH
are trade marks of Oxford University Press

ISBN 0 19 432361 7

Typeset by Pentacor PLC, High Wycombe, Bucks
Printed in Hong Kong

The authors would like to acknowledge the help and cooperation of the
following schools in the production of this course:

Anglo European Study Tours, Abon Language School, Bristol;
Centro Europeo de Idiomas, Valencia;
IHSP, Bromley; ITS Hastings; King's School, Beckenham; The British
Institute, Valencia

and the following people at Oxford University Press:

Alison Findlay, Coralie Green, Yvonne de Henseler, Jean Hindmarch,
Claire Nicholl, Rosy Nixon, James Richardson, Greg Sweetnam,
Andy Younger.

Special thanks also go to Paul Power, Fiona Wright and Simon Taylor.

The publishers would like to thank the following for their permission
to reproduce photographs:

Alton Towers Leisure Park, Anthony Blake, The Bettman Archive,
Britain on View, Colorific!, Sally and Richard Greenhill, Popperfoto,
Rex Features Ltd

and the following for their time and assistance:

Barclays Bank, Oxford; The Eckersley School of English; The Ferry
Sports Centre, Oxford; New Marston Post Office; Oxford Railway
Station; A Watson and Son Ltd.

Location and studio photography by:

Catherine Blackie, Rob Judges, Mark Mason.

Illustrations by:

Jacqueline Bisset, Kate Charlesworth, Susannah English, Maggie
Ling, Andrew MacConville, Mohsen John Modaberi, Bill Piggins,
Christine Roche, Paul Thomas, Brian Walker.

CONTENTS

UNIT	LESSON I	LESSON 2	LESSON 3
	GRAMMAR IN ACTION	ENGLISH IN SITUATIONS	FUN WITH ENGLISH
1 PAGES 6–11	present simple, including *do* construction can/can't *have got* demonstrations	introductions greetings asking for things asking to borrow things saying goodbye	*Further practice in:* pronunciation listening vocabulary reading speaking finding out about the UK
2 PAGES 12–17	present continuous/present simple contrasted future: *going to* *some/any much/many a lot of/a little/a few*	using English money asking about the price of things asking about and telling the time	*Further practice in:* pronunciation listening vocabulary reading speaking finding out about the UK
3 PAGES 18–23	past simple *there was/there were* infinitive of purpose	asking about and describing where buildings/places are accepting and refusing food at mealtimes	*Further practice in:* pronunciation listening vocabulary reading speaking finding out about the UK
4 PAGES 24–29	past simple/past continuous contrasted adverbs of manner	spelling in English apologizing/responding to apologies	*Further practice in:* pronunciation listening vocabulary reading · speaking finding out about the UK
5 PAGES 30–35	present perfect: all uses present perfect/-past simple contrasted	using a payphone and making an international phone call cashing traveller's cheques changing money talking about days and dates	*Further practice in:* pronunciation listening vocabulary reading speaking finding out about the UK
6 PAGES 36–41	comparatives superlatives *not as . . . as*	*buying clothes* *talking about sizes and colours*	*Further practice in:* pronunciation listening vocabulary reading speaking finding out about the UK

UNIT	LESSON 1 GRAMMAR IN ACTION	LESSON 2 ENGLISH IN SITUATIONS	LESSON 3 FUN WITH ENGLISH
7 PAGES 42–47	future: *will* first conditional	using the telephone telephone numbers taking messages on the telephone	*Further practice in:* pronunciation listening vocabulary reading speaking finding out about the UK
8 PAGES 48–53	*who / which* various uses of the gerund	using public transport	*Further practice in:* pronunciation listening vocabulary reading speaking finding out about the UK
9 PAGES 54–59	tag questions *to suppose / think so* *to tell / want / ask* *(someone to do something)*	asking permission inviting and making offers accepting / refusing invitations and offers apologizing and making excuses	*Further practice in:* pronunciation listening vocabulary reading speaking finding out about the UK
10 PAGES 60–65	second conditional *somebody / anybody /* *something / anything*	*talking about parts of the body* *asking / saying what's the matter* *at the doctor's*	*Further practice in:* pronunciation listening vocabulary reading speaking finding out about the UK
11 PAGES 66–71	passives	talking about rules and obligations	*Further practice in:* pronunciation listening vocabulary reading speaking finding out about the UK
12 PAGES 72–77	revision	saying goodbye thanking revision	*Further practice in:* pronunciation listening vocabulary reading speaking finding out about the UK

UNIT ONE · LESSON ONE

A *What's your surname?*
B *Hierro.*
A *How do you spell that?*
B *H–I–E–R–R–O.*
A *How old are you?*
B *I'm seventeen.*

C *Where are you from?*
D *I'm from Brazil.*
C *Where in Brazil?*
D *From Recife, in the north.*

E *What languages do you speak?*
F *Dutch, and a bit of German.*
  And English, of course. But I can't
  speak it very well.
E *Don't worry. Neither can I.*

G *Have you got any brothers or sisters?*
H *Yes, I've got one brother and two*
  sisters. This is my brother ... and
  these are my sisters. How about you?
G *I've only got one brother.*

I *What are you interested in? I mean,*
  what do you do in your free time?
J *Well, I like rock music.*
I *So do I.*
J *And I'm interested in programming.*
I *What's that?*
J *I write programs for computers.*
I *Really? I don't know anything about*
  computers.
J *Don't you? Do you want me to tell*
  you about them? . . .

First lesson, first day

1 Questions and answers

a Match the questions on the left with the answers on the right.

Example: 1 – d

1 What's your first name?	a) 17.
2 What's your family name?	b) Gothenburg, on the west coast.
3 How do you spell that?	c) Yes, I've got one brother.
4 How old are you?	d) Peter.
5 Where are you from?	e) Swedish, of course, and English.
6 Where in *Sweden*?	f) Ekberg.
7 What languages do you speak?	g) No, I haven't.
8 Have you got any brothers or sisters?	h) Sweden.
9 Have you got a photo of *him*?	i) Ice hockey and tennis.
10 What are you interested in?	j) E–K–B–E–R–G.

b Work in pairs. Student A asks Student B questions to fill in the table. Change roles.

c Tell the class about the student you spoke to.

First name:	
Family name:	
Age:	
Nationality:	
Languages:	
Brothers/Sisters:	
Interests:	

2 Find out

a Sit next to a student you don't know very well. Ask each other questions to find six things you have in common. Ask questions like these:

Are you . . . ?

Do you | *like . . . ?*
| *live in . . . ?*
| *go to . . . ?*

Can you | *play . . . ?*
| *speak . . . ?*

Have you got | *a . . . ?*
| *any . . . ?*

b Write down the six things you have in common.

Examples:
Marco lives in a flat, and so do I.
He doesn't like spaghetti, and neither do I.
He's got a girlfriend, and so have I.
He hasn't got a computer, and neither have I.
He can speak a bit of French, and so can I.
He can't play billiards, and neither can I.

3 Quick questions

Form two teams (if possible boys in one team, and girls in the other). In five minutes, talk to as many students as you can find from the other group. Try to find students:

- whose first names begin with the same letter as yours
- whose family names end with the same letter as yours
- whose birthdays are in the same month as yours
- who've got the same number of brothers/sisters as you
- who are interested in the same sport as you
- whose favourite singer or group is the same as yours
- who've got a £10 note in their pockets.

4 Who's who?

a Look at the pictures of six different people. Guess what countries they come from, how old they are, and what jobs they have. Write your answers in the table.

Choose from the information in the box.

18	24	22	16	21	26

bank clerk   rock singer   journalist
factory worker   teacher   student

Spanish   Italian   German
Swedish   French   Brazilian

	Nationality	Age	Job
A			
B			
C			
D			
E			
F			

b Work in pairs. Compare your answers.

Examples:
A *What nationality do you think he is?*
B *I think he looks German.*
A *So do I.*
B *How old do you think he is?*
A *I think he's 22.*
B *I think he's 26.*
A *What do you think he does?*
B *I think he looks like a bank clerk.*

c 🖵 Now listen to the cassette, and check that you have written the correct answers.

Grammar summary: page 82

7

1 Introductions

Hi. I'm Michelle.

Hello. My name's Dieter.

Um . . . this is Hans.

Hi Ans. Nice to meet you.

No, not Ans – Hans.

Oh, I'm sorry. H–H–Hans! !

a Practise the dialogue in groups of three using the same names.

b Form different groups of three. Practise the dialogue again but use your own names. (One of you must make a mistake with a name.)

Note: In formal situations you may hear adults say, 'How do you do?' The answer is, 'How do you do?' or 'Pleased to meet you.'

2 Greetings

a Practise the dialogue in pairs using your own names. Change roles.

b Move around the class. Greet at least three different students. Change the underlined phrases to:

A	B
How are things?	*All right, thanks.*
How's it going?	*Very well, thanks.*
How's life?	*Not too bad, thanks.*

3 Asking for things

Hi, Tina. How are you?

Fine thanks. How are you?

OK thanks.

£2.85

30P

PEPSI

Can Could	I have . . . please?	Yes, here you are. Yes, of course. Yes, anything else?

Herbal Shampoo or dry hair

£1.9

500ml

£1.75

95p

30p

a Work in pairs. Ask each other for the things in the pictures.

Example:
A *Can I have a stamp, please?*
B *Yes, anything else?*
A *No, thanks. How much is that?*
B *30p.*

b Now think of similar things and their prices. Ask each other for them in the same way.

4 Numbers dictation

a Listen and write down the numbers you hear.

Examples: *50   115*

b Listen and write down the prices you hear.

Examples: *20p   £2.50*

5 What do they want?

 Listen to the cassette. Tick the things which each person asks for and how much they cost.

1 ☐ coffee ☐ black ☐ 35p
   ☐ tea   ☐ white ☐ 45p
                      ☐ 54p

2 ☐ Coca-cola ☐ regular   ☐ 34p
   ☐ Pepsi-cola ☐ diet   ☐ 44p
   ☐ Seven-up   ☐ sugar-free ☐ 45p

3 ☐ egg   ☐ white ☐ 57p
   ☐ cheese   ☐ brown ☐ 65p
   ☐ ham   ☐ 72p
   ☐ cheese & tomato   ☐ 78p

4 ☐ egg & chips   ☐ 95p
   ☐ sausage & chips   ☐ £1.15
   ☐ sausage, egg & chips ☐ £1.25
   ☐ sausage & baked beans ☐ £1.35

6 Asking to borrow things

Can	I borrow . . . please?	Yes, of course.
Could	you lend me . . . please?	Yes, here you are.
		No, I'm sorry . . .
		No, I'm afraid not . .

a Work in pairs. Student A asks to borrow the things in the pictures, student B answers.

Example:
A *Can I borrow your pen, please?*
B *Yes, here you are.*

B *Could you lend me your bicycle, please?*
A *No, I'm sorry. It's not working.*

b Go round the class asking to borrow different things from other students as above.

7  Saying goodbye

Boy *Goodbye then.*
Girl *Yeah, cheers, bye.*

(pause)

Are you still there?
Boy *Yes. Are you?*
Girl *Yes.*

(pause)

I must go now. Cheerio.
Boy *Yes, see you tomorrow. Bye.*
Girl *Bye bye . . .*

(long pause)

Hello . . . ?

a Practise the dialogue in pairs. Change roles.

b Go round the class saying goodbye to other students. Use these words and phrases:

Bye.	See you	later.
Bye bye.		tomorrow.
Goodbye.		soon.
Cheerio.		on (Saturday).
Cheers.		
See you.		

Summary of English in situations

- introducing yourself and other people
- greeting people
- asking for things
- asking to borrow things
- saying goodbye

1 Sound right

a Find words on the right which rhyme with those on the left. Write them in the boxes below.

1	court	climb
2	turn	steal
3	through	which
4	own	fire
5	moon	break
6	sun	noun
7	rich	phone
8	time	would
9	make	one
10	feel	sport
11	higher	shoe
12	good	learn
13	brown	tune

b Which word can you read downwards?

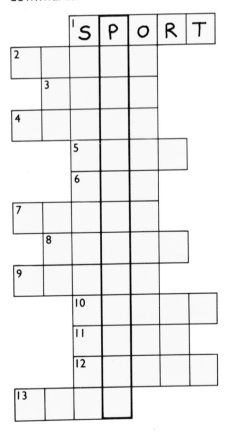

c 🎞 Now listen to the words on the cassette and repeat them.

2 Read and think

Who's who?

There are six students in a language class. Work out where each of them sits.

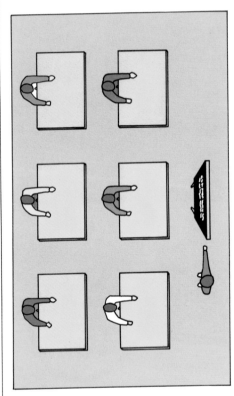

- A is a boy. His name's Pierre. He speaks French.
- B is a girl. Her name's Steffi.
- C is a boy. His name's Sergio, and he's Italian.
- D is also a boy. He's Spanish.
- E is a girl. She speaks Greek, and her name's Sofia.
- F is also a girl. She's Swedish.

- In the front row there are two boys.
- Pierre sits next to the Swedish girl, on her left.
- Steffi is German.
- The Italian boy sits between a German girl and a Greek girl.
- The Greek girl sits on the right.
- The French boy sits in front of Steffi.
- Anna sits next to José.
- In the second row there are two girls.

3 Listen to this

Picture dictation

a 🎞 Listen to the descriptions of two pictures and draw the pictures on two pieces of paper. Start your pictures like this:

Picture 1

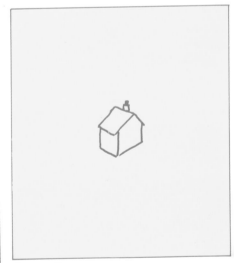

Picture 2

b Work in pairs. Don't let your partner see your pictures. Student A describes what is in his/her picture 1, student B checks that his/her picture is the same.

c Student B describes what is in his/her picture 2 and student A checks that his/her picture is the same.

4 Work on words

Put the words below into the correct column.

Sitting room	Kitchen	Bathroom	Bedroom	Anywhere inside	Outside
	fridge				

fridge shower mirror cooker sofa freezer ashtray sink cushions
dishwasher gate ceiling steps wardrobe towel carpet cupboards
armchair roof wash basin fireplace duvet fence plants floor hangers
path pillows chimney wallpaper drawers lamp shelves taps sheets
microwave lawn flowerbed shed hedge razor toothbrush bookcase

5 Time to talk

a Form groups. You are going to write a questionnaire to help people find their 'perfect' partner.

Example:

Do you prefer boys / girls with:
- ☐ a) long hair
- ☐ b) short hair
- ☐ c) medium-length hair?

In the evening do you prefer to:
- ☐ a) go out
- ☐ b) stay home and watch television
- ☐ c) go to bed early?

Are you:
- ☐ a) talkative
- ☐ b) shy
- ☐ c) generous
- ☐ d) intellectual?

b When you have finished your questionnaire try it out on people in the other groups.

6 Play games in English

Quick 'pix'

a Form two teams. One member of each team stands at the blackboard.

b The teacher says a letter. Each of the two students at the blackboard quickly draws a picture of something beginning with that letter. His/her team must guess what it is. The first team to guess get a point.

c Another member of each team stands at the blackboard, etc.

7 Now you're here

a Ask someone who lives in this town / area the questions below.

1 How many people live here?
2 How old is it?
3 What's the main industry?
4 Has anybody famous ever lived here?
5 What's the political party of the local MP?
6 What's the best football team?
7 Which day is early closing day?
8 Where do young people go on Saturday night?
9 Which is the best pub?
10 What time do the pubs close?
11 Is there much unemployment?
12 Is there much vandalism?
13 What times do banks / shops open and close?
14 Where is the nearest:
   post office?
   railway station?
   bus station?
15 What do you like best about this town / area?
16 Which of the following are there in this town / area?
   a library ☐
   a sports centre ☐
   a hospital ☐
   a cinema ☐
   a theatre ☐
   a museum ☐
   a football ground ☐
   an airport ☐
   a riding school ☐
   tennis courts ☐
   a concert hall ☐
   an amusement arcade ☐
   a mosque ☐
   a university ☐
   a castle ☐
   an ice-rink ☐
   a bowling alley ☐
   a swimming pool ☐

b Compare your answers in class.

GRAMMAR IN ACTION

🖼 Easy money?

In Britain, students who need some extra money often get temporary summer jobs in seaside towns like Bournemouth.

Jessica Wilson is working in a bed and breakfast—a small guest house.

Interviewer *How many hours do you work?*
Jessica *A lot! Seven or eight hours a day, six days a week. It's very hard work, compared to school!*
Interviewer *What do you do?*
Jessica *I start work at seven o'clock—before I'm really awake! I make breakfast—a real English breakfast with cereals, toast, fried egg, bacon, sausage, tomato, and tea or coffee. I can't understand how people can eat so much so early in the morning—I don't have any breakfast myself, just a cup of coffee.*

I'm glad I'm not going to eat this!

Interviewer *What do you do then?*
Jessica *I wash up. There are a lot of greasy plates after an English breakfast.*

I'm trying to get the grease off this plate!

Interviewer *What do you do after breakfast?*
Jessica *I hoover. Some people complain that the noise wakes them up—at half past ten!*
Interviewer *Do you clean the rooms too?*
Jessica *Yes, as soon as the guests leave their rooms, I go in. First I change the sheets and make the beds. Then I tidy the room. After that I clean the bath, and put the cap on the toothpaste—you know, little things like that.*

I'm going to wake them up—it's almost 11 o'clock!

Interviewer *How do guests leave their rooms?*
Jessica *Well, a few people leave their rooms nice and tidy, and there isn't much to do. But some people make a terrible mess. They leave rubbish everywhere—especially under the bed!*

I'm not really enjoying this!

Interviewer *Do you like your job?*
Jessica *Yes and no. I don't enjoy the washing-up—breakfast dishes always have a little egg yolk left on them, and it's very difficult to get it off. But I enjoy some things—I meet a lot of interesting people, especially foreigners. I can practise my French with some of them.*

Qu'est-ce-que tu vas faire ce soir?

Sorry?

What are you going to do this evening?

Interviewer *How much do you earn?*
Jessica *Not much.*
Interviewer *Do you get any tips?*
Jessica *Yes, a few. They're the best part of the job.*

1 Questions and answers

a Put *much* or *many* in the gaps in the questions.

b Answer the questions using the phrases in the table.

c Ask and answer the questions in pairs.

How	...	1 hours a day does Jessica work? 2 days a week does she work? 3 money does she earn? 4 greasy plates does she wash? 5 people are still asleep at 10.30? 6 food do English people eat for breakfast? 7 does Jessica eat for breakfast?	A lot. Not much. Not many.
	...	8 guests leave their rooms in a mess? 9 guests leave their rooms nice and tidy? 10 rubbish does Jessica find under the beds? 11 interesting people does she meet? 12 French does she speak? 13 tips does she get?	A little. A few.

2 What's Jessica doing?

a 🔊 Listen to the sounds on the cassette and write down what Jessica's doing.

Example:
She's making a bed.

1 ....
2 ....
3 ....
4 ....
5 ....
6 ....
7 ....

b Check your answers in pairs.

Example:
A *What's Jessica doing in number 1?*
B *She's ...*

3 What am I doing?

a Form two teams, A and B.

b For five minutes, each team makes a list of instructions.

Examples:
Fasten your seat belt in a car.
Hide under a bed.
Get onto an elephant's back.

c A student from team A looks at the first instruction on team B's list. He / She then stands at the front of the class and mimes the instruction. Team A try to guess what he / she is doing.

d A student from team B looks at the first instruction on team A's list, etc.

4 What are they going to do?

Work in pairs. Student A looks at this page. Student B turns to page 78.

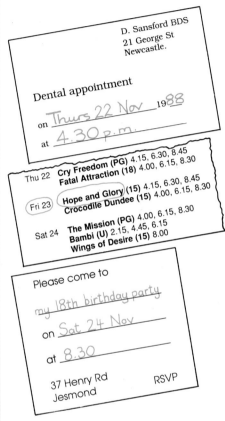

a Student B is going to ask you what you are going to do next week. Answer the questions. Use your own ideas if necessary.

b Now ask student B similar questions.

Examples:
A *What are you going to do next week?*
B *I'm going to the cinema.*
A *What are you going to see? / Who are you going with?*

c Now write down what you are *really* going to do over the next few days. Ask B what he / she is going to do. Then answer B's questions.

Grammar summary: page 82

13

1 Using English money

How much is this?

a Work in pairs. Ask and answer questions about each picture.

Example:
A *How much is this?*
B *It's £1.34.*

1

2

3

4

b Now do the same with your English money.

The money game

Look at these things. What is the minimum number of coins you need to pay for these things exactly?

Example: 27p
three coins—20p, 5p and 2p

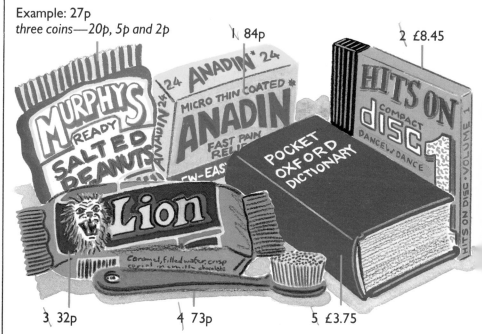

1 84p
2 £8.45
3 32p
4 73p
5 £3.75

2 How much are they?

A *How much is a Lion Bar, please?*
B *32p.*
A *And can I have a packet of peanuts, please?*
B *That's 59p altogether, please.*
A *Thanks.*

a Practise the dialogue in pairs.

b Student A 'buys' one or two of the things above as in the example. Use real money if you've got some. A must check his/her change.

3 What's missing?

📺 Listen to the conversation in a shop. Write down:

1 the five things the girl buys
2 what each of them costs
3 the total cost.

4 Act it out

a Work in pairs. Student A is a customer and wants to buy four things. Student B is a shop assistant in a chemist's shop and tells student A what the things cost.

b Student B is a customer who wants to buy four things in a newsagent's. Student A is a shop assistant and tells A what the things cost.

5 Prices

A How much is a <u>Mars Bar</u> in Spain?
B About 75 pesetas.
A How much is that in English money?
B About 40p.

Work in pairs. Talk about your country and use the words in the box instead of the underlined words.

a litre of petrol
a litre of milk
an LP
a hamburger
a local call from a public telephone box
a cup of coffee in a cafe
a local newspaper
a 50cc moped
a pair of Levi jeans

6 Asking about and telling the time

A Excuse me. Can you tell me the time, please?
B Yes, it's half past ten.
A Thanks very much.

A Have you got the time, please?
B Yes, it's exactly thirteen minutes past eight.
A Thanks.

A What's the time, please?
B Sorry?
A What time is it, please?
B Ah, it's twenty-five to six.

What's the time?

Work in pairs. Take it in turns to ask and say what time it is. Use the same questions as in the three dialogues above.

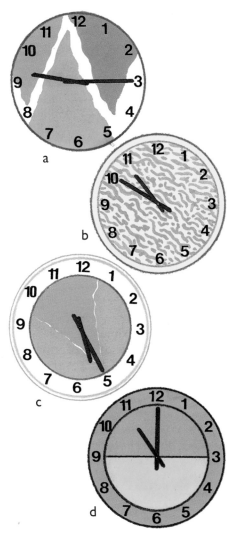

a

b

c

d

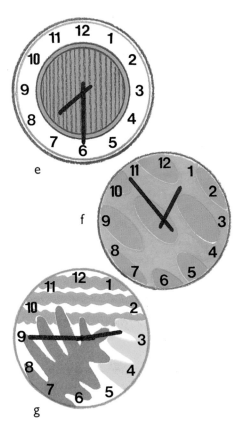

e

f

g

7 What time is it?

Listen to the short conversations and announcements. Write down the time which is mentioned in each of them.

1 4.15
2 ....
3 ....
4 ....
5 ....
6 ....
7 ....

Summary of English in situations

● asking and talking about the price of things
● asking about and telling the time

1 Sound right

a Which word does not rhyme with the other two?

Example:
catch (watch) match

1	slow	know	now
2	but	put	cut
3	good	could	food
4	great	wait	seat
5	here	their	there
6	worry	hurry	sorry
7	three	grey	key
8	our	your	four
9	does	goes	toes
10	quite	quiet	right

b Now practise saying the words above.

c Think of one other word which rhymes with each pair of rhyming words.

2 Listen to this

Listen to the short conversations on the cassette and write down what the people are talking *about*.

1 ....

2 ....

3 ....

4 ....

5 ....

6 ....

7 ....

8 ....

9 ....

3 Read and think

What's on?

a Read the notices below, and then answer the questions.

THE SHELDONIAN THEATRE

THE CHURCHILL PLAY
by Howard Brenton

"Brilliant"
G. P. Lewis,
Sunday Review

Weekdays: 8.00pm
Sunday: 7.30pm
Stalls: £7.50
Circle: £9.00
Reservations: Tel 723055

FINAL WEEK!

Karma
Health Food Restaurant
5 Castle Street

Hot and cold vegetarian food

Lunch (12.00 - 4.00):
Self-service

Dinner (7.00 - 11.00):
Table service

For bookings ring:
0865 - 53060

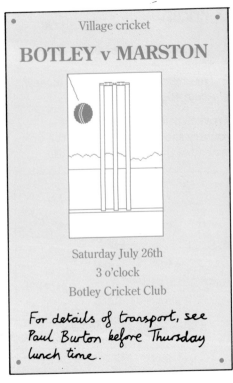

Village cricket

BOTLEY v MARSTON

Saturday July 26th
3 o'clock
Botley Cricket Club

For details of transport, see Paul Burton before Thursday lunch time.

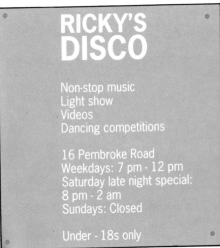

RICKY'S DISCO

Non-stop music
Light show
Videos
Dancing competitions

16 Pembroke Road
Weekdays: 7 pm - 12 pm
Saturday late night special:
8 pm - 2 am
Sundays: Closed

Under - 18s only

1 What is the maximum age for people who want to go dancing?
2 When is there self-service at the Karma restaurant?
3 If you like Howard Brenton's play, you should go to the theatre as soon as possible. Why?
4 When do you have to decide if you want to go to the cricket match?
5 Is the disco open every night of the week?
6 Which theatre seats are more expensive – stalls or circle?
7 What kind of food do you get at Karma?
8 Who is organizing the trip to Botley?
9 What is the latest time Ricky's Disco is open to?
10 What can you do if you want to be sure to get a table for dinner at Karma?

b Now think of three more questions about the notices. Ask each other the questions in groups.

4 Work on words

a Which of these words is different from the other four?

b Why is it different?

Example:

pink
mauve
(pale)
purple
grey

It is different because it is *not* a colour.

1	cabbage	6	wine
	lettuce		beer
	onion		lager
	plum		fruit juice
	carrot		cider
2	chicken	7	pears
	cow		bananas
	pig		grapes
	sheep		peas
	goat		peaches
3	uncle	8	scooter
	nephew		moped
	aunt		bicycle
	brother		motorbike
	grandfather		car
4	breakfast	9	butter
	meal		milk
	dinner		cheese
	lunch		meat
	supper		yoghurt
5	cup	10	avenue
	glass		path
	mug		road
	plate		street
	vase		motorway

5 Time to talk

What are you afraid of?

a Answer the questions below. Write 1, 2, 3 or 4 in each box.

1 = Not at all.   3 = Yes, quite.
2 = No, not really.   4 = Yes, very.

Are you afraid of:

☐ spiders?   ☐ mice?
☐ snakes?   ☐ the dark?
☐ blood?   ☐ thunder?
☐ heights?

b Compare your answers in groups. Try to explain *why* you are afraid of certain things.

c Tell the group about any other things you are afraid of.

6 Play games in English

Add a verb

a Form two teams, A and B.

b The teacher writes a noun up on the board.

c A student from each team writes a verb connected with that noun until one team cannot think of another verb.

d The teacher then writes up a new word (a noun).
Example:
a car: drive   buy   wash   repair   crash

7 Now you're here

Ask someone from this town / area these questions:

a Which of these shops are in this town / area?

b What sort of things do they sell?

1	Next	☐	....
2	Boots	☐	....
3	WH Smith	☐	....
4	Tesco	☐	....
5	Marks and Spencer	☐	....
6	Halfords	☐	....
7	Etam	☐	....
8	Dolcis	☐	....
9	C & A	☐	....
10	Sainsbury	☐	....
11	B & Q	☐	....
12	The Body Shop	☐	....
13	BHS	☐	....
14	Dixons	☐	....
15	Ravel	☐	....
16	Currys	☐	....
17	Habitat	☐	....
18	Thomas Cook	☐	....
19	Laura Ashley	☐	....
20	Benetton	☐	....
21	Maynards	☐	....

c Find out how much each of these things cost. Write down the name of the shop where you see each thing for sale.

1 a pint of milk
2 a local evening newspaper
3 a Mars Bar
4 cod and chips in a fish and chip shop
5 a stamp for a postcard to your country
6 a packet of Smith's cheese and onion crisps
7 a cinema ticket
8 a single in the Top Twenty
9 a tube of Colgate fluoride
10 one play on a juke box
11 entry to a disco
12 developing and printing a film
13 a C90 blank tape
14 dry cleaning a jacket

UNIT THREE

LESSON ONE

GRAMMAR IN ACTION

For sale: Old phone boxes

A rich English film star in Hollywood felt homesick, so she bought one—to remind her of home and to use as a bar.

A man from Yorkshire wanted somewhere to keep his fifty racing pigeons.

Not long ago, there were red telephone boxes everywhere in Britain. But then British Telecom decided to get rid of these old-fashioned boxes. A lot of people were angry because they didn't like the new aluminium and glass boxes. So BT agreed to keep a few of the old, traditional boxes and sell the rest— 60,000 of them—for between £200 and £2,000.

But who wanted to buy an old telephone box, and why? Different people had different reasons.

A couple from Manchester got fed up because their son had endless telephone conversations with his girlfriend. For his eighteenth birthday, they gave him his own phone box, so they could watch television in peace.

A couple from Bristol thought it was the perfect place for their daughter to practise her violin.

A woman from Devon had too many tropical fish for her small tank, so she bought a phone box to use as an aquarium.

A millionaire from Brighton needed a changing room for the swimming pool in his garden (he put in one-way glass of course!).

A man from north London gave his wife a phone box as a wedding present. Why? Because one day he waited outside a phone box for a long, long time. There was a woman inside. Finally he knocked on the window, and she came out. He spoke to her, and that night they went out together. Two months later, he rang her from the same phone box to ask her to marry him. She said 'yes' just in time—before his money ran out.

18

I Make true sentences

Make sentences from the three columns. Put the verbs in the middle column in the past simple.

Example:
The old phone boxes were red.

I The old phone boxes	(sell)	a) one-way glass in his box.
2 British Telecom	(have)	b) their son a phone box.
3 A man from Yorkshire	(give)	c) red.
4 A woman from Devon	(think)	d) a box for his pigeons.
5 An English film star	(buy)	e) too many fish.
6 A couple from Manchester	(be)	f) to the woman in the phone box.
7 The boy from Manchester	(put)	g) a lot of old phone boxes.
8 The man from north London	(feel)	h) homesick in Hollywood.
9 The couple from Bristol	(have)	i) endless conversations with his girlfriend.
10 The millionaire from Brighton	(speak)	j) it was a perfect place to practise the violin.

2 What's wrong?

This is a picture of an English family at home a hundred years ago. There are a lot of mistakes in the picture.

a Work in teams and make a list of the mistakes.

Examples:
There weren't any televisions 100 years ago.
People didn't wear jeans.

b Team A read out the first 'mistake' on their list. Team B cross it off their list if they've got it. Team B then read out the first 'mistake' on their list, etc.

The team with the longest remaining list wins. If a team says something which is *not* a 'mistake', they lose one point.

3 Things to remember

a This is Kathy's first day on holiday. Yesterday was a very busy day for her. Look at the map and Kathy's list. Then ask and answer questions about her in pairs.

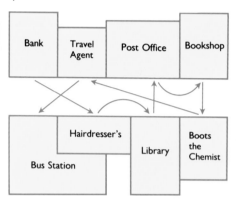

Example:
A *Where did she go first?*
B *She went to the bank to get some traveller's cheques.*
A *What did she do after that?*
B *She . . .*

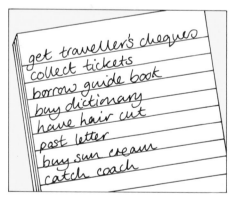

get traveller's cheques
collect tickets
borrow guide book
buy dictionary
have hair cut
post letter
buy sun cream
catch coach

b Now think back to the day(s) before you came to Britain. What things did you do to prepare for your trip to Britain? Which places did you go to and why? Think of six things.

Examples:
I went to my grandmother's to say goodbye.
I packed my suitcase.

Compare your lists in groups.

Grammar summary: page 83

19

1 Describing where buildings / places are

Match the pictures with the phrases in the box.

it's on the corner of . . .
go straight on
it's between . . .
it's opposite . . .
turn left
take the second turning on the right
it's at the end of . . .
it's next to . . .
go past
it's on the other side of . . .

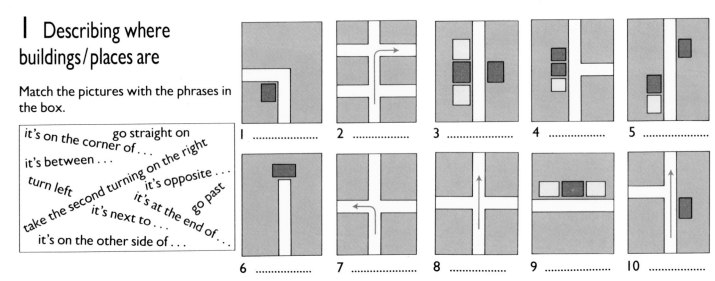

1 ....   2 ....   3 ....   4 ....   5 ....

6 ....   7 ....   8 ....   9 ....   10 ....

2 Where do they want to go?

Listen to the three conversations on the cassette. They all take place at the bus station (X). Follow the directions you hear and draw arrows (→ → →) on the map. Where does each person want to go?

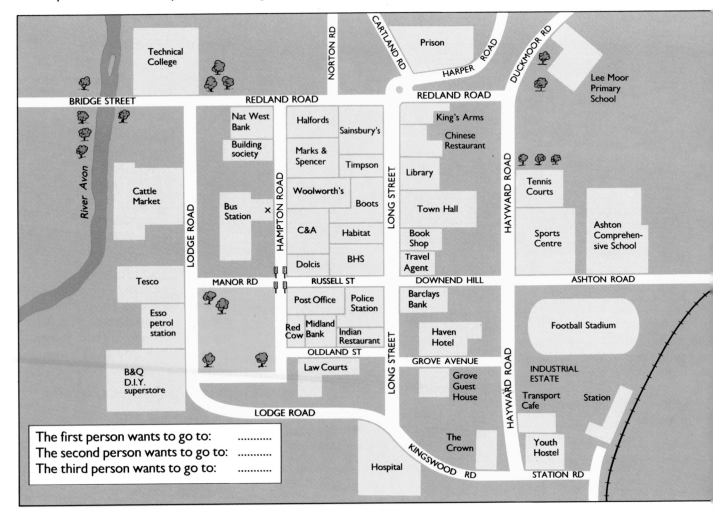

The first person wants to go to: ....
The second person wants to go to: ....
The third person wants to go to: ....

3 Ask and answer

Work in pairs. You are at X on the map. Student A asks how to get to another place on the map. Student B describes how to get there. Change roles.

Use phrases like:

A *Can you tell me where . . . is, please?*
Can you tell me the way to . . . , please?

B *Yes, go down this street. Take the first turning on the left . . .*

A *Thanks.*
Thanks a lot.
Thanks very much.
Thank you very much.

B *That's all right.*
That's OK.
You're welcome.

4 What's missing?

Work in pairs. Student A looks at the map below. Student B looks at the map on page 78.

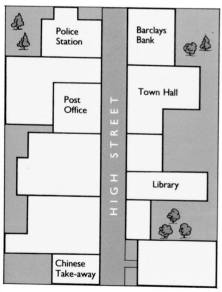

You want to know were these places/ buildings are:
1 the tennis courts
2 the Bear (pub)

3 the bus station
4 Tesco's supermarket
5 a fish and chip shop
6 the Churchill Hotel.

Find and mark them on your map with the information you get from student B. Take it in turns to ask and answer questions. (Student A starts.)

5 🖭 What to say at mealtimes

A *Is that enough meat for you?*
B *Yes thanks, that's fine . . .*
Um, can I have a drink, please?
A *Yes, of course. Help yourself to a glass of water.*
C *More potatoes?*
B *Yes, please.*
A *Have you got enough beans?*
B *Yes, thanks.*
C *Would you like some cabbage?*
B *No, thanks.*
A *Please start. Don't wait for me.*

    (pause)

B *Could you pass the salt, please?*
C *Yes, here you are.*
Do you want some gravy?
B *No, thanks.*

    (later)

A *Would you like some more?*
B *No thanks. That was very nice.*
A *Are you sure?*
B *Yes, quite sure thanks. It was lovely but I'm full.*

a Work in groups of three. Read the dialogue. Change roles.

b Act out the situation without looking in the book. Choose from the food and drink in the box, if you want to.

salad dressing	ketchup	pepper
cauliflower	carrots	milk
spinach	sprouts	squash
orange juice	sauce	salad
mustard	peas	chips

6 What *not* to say

In this conversation, B is not very polite. What mistakes does he/she make? Work in pairs and correct them.

A *What would you like to drink?*
B *I want some water.*
A *Would you like some sprouts?*
B *Yes.*
A *Is that enough?*
B *No.*
A *Please start.*
B *Give me the salt.*
A *Yes, of course. Here you are. Pepper?*
B *No.*

    (later)

A *Would you like some chips?*
B *OK.*

    (later)

A *Would you like some more?*
B *Um . . . No.*
A *Are you sure?*
B *Of course.*

Summary of English in situations

- describing where buildings/ places are
- asking for directions
- accepting and refusing food at mealtimes

1 Sound right

a Listen to these words on the cassette. What sound do they all end with?

looked   watched   liked   worked

b Listen again and repeat. Make sure all the words end with the sound [t].

c Now listen to these words. What sound do they all end with?

opened   listened   happened   answered

d Listen again and repeat. Make sure all the words end with the sound [d].

e Now listen to these words. What sound do they all end with?

visited   started   wanted   needed

f Listen again and repeat. Make sure all the words end with the sound [ɪd].

g Now listen to these words on the tape and tick (√) them according to how -ed is pronounced.

	[t]	[d]	[ɪd]
1 pushed			
2 borrowed			
3 hated			
4 turned			
5 washed			
6 landed			
7 stopped			
8 changed			
9 posted			

h Now practise pronouncing the same words in the correct way.

2 Listen to this

a Listen to the three conversations which took place on a shopping trip. Number the shops which the girl went into, 1–3.

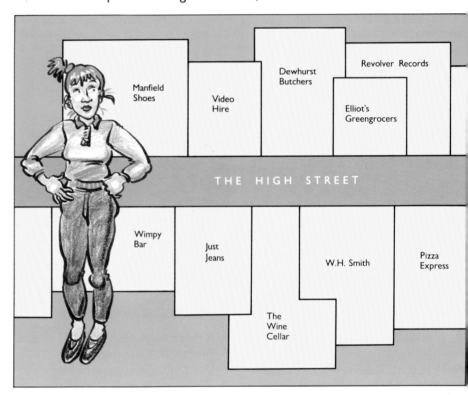

b Answer these questions.

1 How much did she spend in the first shop?
2 What did she buy?
3 How much did she spend in the second shop?
4 What did she buy?
5 How much did she spend in the third shop?
6 What did she buy?
7 How much did she spend altogether?

3 Time to talk

a Form two to four groups.

b In 3 minutes write down as many uses as you can of the first object in the box.

Example:
You can play football with it.
You can keep money in it.

c Now compare the uses you thought of with the other groups'. Who thought of the most uses? Who thought of the most original use?

d Now do the same with the other objects in the box.

an empty can of Coke
a paper bag
a mirror
a toothbrush
a brick
a coin
a paperclip
a matchbox

4 Read and think

Can you solve these problems?

1 Andy, Ben and Chris have different jobs. One is a teacher, one is a gardener, and one is a mechanic. But who's who?
- Andy, the shortest, has never met Chris, the tallest.
- Yesterday the mechanic went to see his friend, the gardener. He found that the gardener had gone to the pub with the teacher.
- The teacher's taller than the gardener.

Andy is . . .
Ben is . . .
Chris is . . .

2 In a cinema, four boys are sitting in a row.
- Nick's sitting next to Colin, on his left.
- Daniel's sitting next to Colin, on his right.
- Andrew's sitting to the left of Daniel.

Who's who in the picture?

3 A video has been stolen. There are four suspects, Joe, John, Jane and Jack.
- Joe said, 'It was stolen by a girl.'
- John said, 'No, Jack stole it.'
- Jane said, 'You're lying, John.'
- Jack said, 'I didn't steal it.'

Only one of the statements was false. Who stole the video?

4 There were five cars in a race.
- A did not come first.
- B was neither first nor last.
- C came one place behind A.
- D was not second.
- E was two places behind D.

In which order did the cars come?

5 Work on words

Put the words in the box in the correct column.

disgusting	safe	pleasant
marvellous	ugly	useless
careless	rude	popular
brilliant	tidy	smooth
comfortable	weak	honest
delicious	neat	smelly
enjoyable	smart	clumsy
embarrassing	lucky	boring
miserable	lazy	nasty
disappointing	awful	gentle
successful	brave	bitter
valuable	false	

Positive	Negative
good	bad

6 Play games in English

How many words?

Form two to four teams and make as many words as you can from the word:

INTERNATIONAL

The words must have three letters or more. You must know what the words mean. You must *not* use dictionaries.

You score 1 point for each word on your list. You get an extra point for every word with 5 letters or more.

You get an extra point if you have a word on your list which the other team(s) haven't got. The team with the most points is the winner.

7 Now you're here

Ask a British person the questions below.

1 How much do people with the following jobs earn a year?

    a secondary school teacher
    a police officer
    a farm worker
    a member of parliament
    a nurse
    a coal miner

2 Are women paid the same as men for doing the same job?
3 What jobs are done only by women?
4 What jobs are done only by men?
5 How many people in Britain are unemployed at the moment?
6 How much does a single unemployed person receive on 'the dole'?
7 Where in Britain is it very difficult to find a job?
8 How many weeks' holiday a year does the average person get?
9 At what age do men/women retire?

Compare your answers in class.

UNIT FOUR

LESSON ONE

Absurd but true

Late for the match

Manchester police yesterday stopped a car which was driving at over 100 miles per hour on the M6 motorway. The police asked the driver why he was driving so fast. The driver said he and his four friends were going to a funeral, and they were late.

The police officer who stopped the car, afterwards commented sarcastically, 'I found it a bit difficult to believe their story. They were all wearing Manchester United scarves and hats.'

Thumbs down

A judge yesterday fined 95-kilo rugby player, Mike Brain, £5. The police arrested Brain, a medical student at Leeds University, as he was hitching by the side of the A1.

Brain protested angrily in court. 'I wasn't doing anything wrong! I was only trying to get a lift as quickly as possible.'

When the police arrested him, Brain was wearing a long blond wig, high heels and a mini-skirt.

Man's best friend?

When Mr and Mrs Kahn, of Golders Green, London, went to the theatre, they left their German shepherd dog, Butch, to guard their luxury home. When two burglars broke in and the burglar alarm rang, Butch was waiting for them.

Unfortunately, one of the burglars was a dog-lover, and he quickly made friends with Butch. Then, while the alarm was ringing, and the burglars were stealing cash and jewellery, worth over £10,000, from a safe, Butch lay down in his basket and went to sleep.

When the police arrived twenty minutes later, the burglars had gone. Butch was proudly guarding the empty safe. When the first detective entered the room, Butch immediately attacked her, tore her trousers and bit her in the leg.

I Three interviews

Use the information in the three newspaper stories to complete these interviews. In the second and third interview, you will have to work out the questions first.

Work in pairs. Change roles.

Interview I

Interviewer	*What do you do?*
Mike Brain	. . .
Interviewer	*What are you studying?*
Mike Brain	. . .
Interviewer	*What were you doing when the police arrested you?*
Mike Brain	. . .
Interviewer	*What were you wearing?*
Mike Brain	. . .
Interviewer	*Why were you wearing those things?*

Mike Brain	. . .
Interviewer	*Why were you angry in court?*
Mike Brain	. . .

Interview 2

Interviewer	*Where / you live?*
Mrs Kahn	. . .
Interviewer	*Where / you go on the evening of the robbery?*
Mrs Kahn	. . .
Interviewer	*How / the thieves get into your house?*
Mrs Kahn	. . .
Interviewer	*Why / not Butch attack them?*
Mrs Kahn	. . .
Interviewer	*What / they steal?*
Mrs Kahn	. . .
Interviewer	*What / Butch doing when the police arrived?*

Mrs Kahn	. . .
Interviewer	*What / Butch do?*
Mrs Kahn	. . .

Interview 3

Interviewer	*Why / stop the car?*
Police officer	. . .
Interviewer	*How fast / they (drive) when you (see) them?*
Police officer	. . .
Interviewer	*How many people / in the car?*
Police officer	. . .
Interviewer	*Where / they say they / (go)?*
Police officer	. . .
Interviewer	*Why / you / not believe them?*
Police officer	. . .

2 What were they doing?

When the teacher walked into this classroom, the students were *not* ready for him. What were they all doing?

Look at the picture carefully for one minute and then turn to page 78.

3 What happened?

🔊 Listen to the sounds on the cassette and say what was happening and then what suddenly happened.

Example:
he was having a shower when the phone rang.

4 Well or badly?

a Write down two things which you do *badly,* two things which you do *well,* two things which you do *fast* and two things which you do *slowly.*

b Sit with a person who you know quite well. Take turns at asking questions and try to guess what the other person has written.

Examples:
Do you | speak French badly?
*   * | play tennis well?
*   * | type fast?
*   * | eat slowly?

How many things have you guessed correctly after three minutes?

5 How do they answer?

a Student A goes out of the room. The rest of the class choose one of the adverbs below.

angrily	slowly	nervously
calmly	loudly	suspiciously
sadly	shyly	excitedly
quickly		quietly

b Student A comes back into the room and asks different students different questions.

Examples:
What did you have for breakfast this morning?
What's the time?
Where did you go last night?
How did you come to Britain?

Each student must answer in the same way, for example, *slowly.*

c Student A must guess *how* they answered.

d A different student goes out of the room and the rest of the class choose a new adverb.

Grammar summary: page 84

1 Spelling in English

A *Can I have your name, please?*
B *Björn Öberg.*
A *Oh goodness! I'm sorry, can you spell that, please?*
B *Yes. B–J–O with two dots over it –R–N, that's Björn. Then O with two dots –B–E–R–G.*
A *Björn Öberg. And your address, please?*
B *43 Grosvenor Crescent.*
A *Grosvenor . . . that's G–R–O–S–V–E–N–O–R, isn't it?*
B *Yes, that's right.*
A *Grosvenor Crescent . . . And do you know your postcode?*
B *Yes, it's TN37 4QU.*
A *Right, I think that's all thanks.*

a Practise the dialogue in pairs. Change roles.

b Practise the dialogue again with another student. Use your own names, addresses, and postcodes.

2 What's the word?

Write down the letters you hear spelt. What words do they make?

Example:
C–O–F–F–E–E = coffee

1	....	6	....
2	....	7	....
3	....	8	....
4	....	9	....
5	....	10	....

Now say the words.

3 Spelling game

Form two teams. Each team prepares a list of ten English words which are difficult to spell (without using a dictionary). Ask each other to spell the words. You must know how to spell them yourselves.

Example:
A *How do you spell 'across'?*
B *A–C–R–O–S–S.*
A *Right.*   *(1 point)*
B *How do you spell 'biscuit'?*
A *B–I–S–K–I–T.*
B *Wrong! B–I–S–C–U–I–T.*   *(1 point)*

4 Pass it on

Form groups of three. Student A thinks of a word and writes it down.

He/She then spells (whispers) it to student B.

Student B writes the word down and spells it (but does not say the word) to student C who also writes it down.

A and C then check that they have the same word.

Student B then thinks of a new word.

5 What's missing?

Work in pairs. Student A reads the instructions below. Student B reads the instructions on page 79.

Look at the information about these two people. Answer student B's questions about them.

Name: Eleanor Carnegie
Address: 63 Marquess Road
          Worcester
Postcode: WO37 8HP

Name: Gareth Rees
Address: 18 Llandaff Street
          Caerphilly, Glamorgan
Postcode: CA12 3SR

Now ask student B questions about these two people and fill in the missing information about them. Ask B to spell any difficult words.

Name: ....
Address: ....
Postcode: ....

Name: ....
Address: ....
Postcode: ....

6 Apologizing

a Practise the short dialogue above in pairs. Then use phrases like these:

A	B
Sorry.	*That's all right.*
I'm very sorry.	*Never mind.*
I'm terribly sorry.	*Don't worry.*

b Act out these situations. A must apologize to B, and B must accept the apology using the phrases above. Change roles.

c Work in pairs. Think of other situations where one person apologizes and the other responds. Act them out in front of the class.

<table>
<tr><td>Summary of English
in situations</td></tr>
<tr><td>• spelling in English
• apologizing/responding
  to apologies</td></tr>
</table>

1 Sound right

a The words on the left are all irregular verbs in the past. Find words on the right which rhyme with them and write them in the boxes.

1 could	g	o	o	d		blue
2 caught						made
3 read						bird
4 took						good
5 bought						head
6 knew						foot
7 chose						goal
8 said						short
9 paid						shows
10 stole						for
11 wore						bed
12 heard						four
13 ate						book
14 saw						get
15 put						court

b  Now listen to the cassette and practise pronouncing the pairs of words.

2 Play games in English

a Form two teams, A and B.

b The teacher writes a letter on the board.

c Team A write another letter. Team B then add a third letter and so on until there is a complete word on the board which *cannot* be added to.

d The team which wrote the last letter win a point.

Example:
Teacher R
Team A E
Team B A
Team A D
Team B Y (one point)

e If one team think that the other team are not trying to spell a 'real' word they can, when it's their turn, ask the other team what word they are thinking of. If they have a real word in mind, they win the point. If not, the team who asked win the point and the teacher begins a new round.

3 Work on words

a Form two teams, A and B. Each team chooses a secretary who writes down the pairs of opposites. Find the pairs of opposites in the two boxes.

b The first team to finish is the winner.

Example:
remember   forget

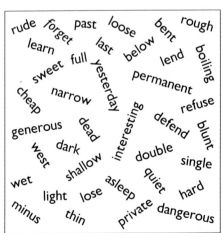

4 Listen to this

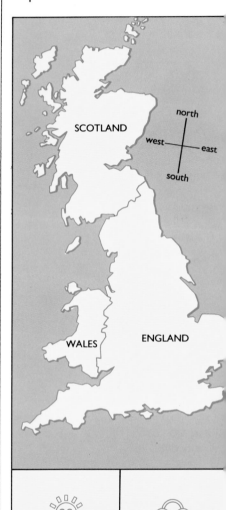 Listen to tomorrow's weather forecast on the cassette and draw the symbols in the correct places on the map.

5 Time to talk

A night at the theatre

Work in pairs. Student A looks at the instructions on this page and student B looks at the instructions on page 79.

Look at the pictures on the right. You have half of a story. Student B has the other half. Your pictures are *not* in the correct order. Describe your pictures to student B. Student B will describe his/her pictures to you. Try to put all twelve pictures in the correct order. Then tell the story between you. You must *not* look at student B's pictures.

6 Read and think

What on earth?

A Match the pictures with the descriptions below. You can use a dictionary if you want to.

1 a trombone player having a bath
2 an ant ski-jumping
3 a dead caterpillar
4 two spiders shaking hands
5 a Mexican on a bicycle
6 a polar bear in a snowstorm
7 a worm trying to climb over a razor blade
8 a bald hedgehog
9 the view from inside an empty beer can
10 a spider blowing bubble gum
11 an elephant caught in a lift
12 a spider falling from a great height
13 a comb for a bald man
14 a giraffe walking past a window
15 a koala bear climbing a tree
16 a porter working, seen from above

B Now draw pictures for the other six descriptions.

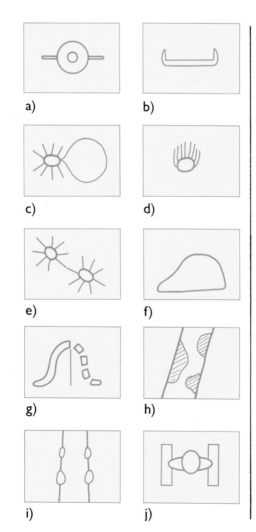

7 Now you're here

Ask a British person these questions or watch a British family at mealtimes and answer them yourselves.

1 What do they have for breakfast?
2 What time do they usually have lunch/the evening meal?
3 What do they call the evening meal?
4 How long do they spend over it?
6 Do they say a prayer before meals?
7 Do they say anything before they start eating?
8 Do they use napkins?
9 What 'foreign' foods do they eat?
10 What do they drink with their main meal of the day?
11 Do they eat bread with that meal?
12 What spices or sauces do they use?
13 How do they leave their knives and forks after a meal?
14 Do they always have a dessert?
15 Do they have cheese/fruit?
16 Do they have coffee?
17 Do they say anything when they leave the table?
18 What things do you find different about British customs at mealtimes?

GRAMMAR IN ACTION

Points of view

The local paper in Torquay, Devon, asked foreign students in the town to write about the strange or unusual things they noticed about Britain. These are some of the replies the paper has received so far.

Dear Sir/Madam

We have been in Torquay for two weeks now. We've met a lot of nice people but we've noticed that people here never touch each other!

Back home in Italy and Spain people always shake hands, hug, and kiss each other on both cheeks when they meet or say goodbye. But here, we have not seen more than half a dozen people shake hands, and we have never seen two people kiss each other on the cheek. But on the other hand, we have noticed the same British people stroke or pat their dogs all the time! Can you explain this?

Yours faithfully,

Pilar Gomez
(Valencia, Spain)
Maria Cassel
(Rome, Italy)

Dear Sir/Madam

I'm an Italian student, and I've been in Britain since June. What's the thing that has surprised me most here? Well, I've noticed that British drivers always stop at red lights and pedestrian crossings!

And another thing — I haven't heard a single car horn yet. Why is this so surprising? The answer to that question is simple — have you ever been to Naples?

Yours,

Ugo Gatti
(Naples, Italy)

Dear Sir/Madam

Since I came to Britain three weeks ago, six people have called me 'dear', ten people have used the word 'darling' to me, and twelve people have told me I'm 'their love'.

Who were all these romantic people? Boyfriends? No, they were all complete strangers, people like bus drivers, shop assistants and police officers. Who says the British aren't friendly?

Love,
Rebeca Guerrios
(Brazil)

1 Three interviews

Interview the foreign students who wrote the letters to the Torquay newspaper. In the second and third interview you must work out the questions first.

Work in pairs. Change roles.

Interview 1

Interviewer *How long have you been in Torquay?*
Pilar . . .
Interviewer *Have you met any nice people?*
Maria . . .

Interviewer *What do people in Spain do when they meet each other?*
Pilar . . .
Interviewer *And what do British people do when they meet?*
Pilar . . .
Interviewer *But haven't you seen any British people kiss each other?*
Maria . . .

Interview 2

Interviewer *How long / you / in Britain?*
Ugo . . .
Interviewer *What / you / notice?*
Ugo . . .

Interviewer *— / anything else / surprise / you?*
Ugo . . .

Interview 3

Interviewer *— / long / you / here?*
Rebeca . . .
Interviewer *— / British people / friendly to you?*
Rebeca . . .
Interviewer *What / they / call / you?*
Rebeca . . .
Interviewer *Who / these people?*
Rebeca . . .

2 Listen to this

🖼 Listen to some short comments on Britain from other foreign visitors. Write down the nationality of the speaker and what he/she is talking about.

	Nationality	Subject
1	French	meals
2		
3		
4		
5		
6		
7		

3 The things you've done

a Work in pairs. Ask each other questions.

* Have you had fish and chips yet? (Did you like it?)
* How many letters/postcards have you written?
* Have you seen any good films or watched any good television programmes? (Which ones? Did you understand them?)
* Have you had any problems since you came? (What kind of problems?)
* Have you got lost? (When? What happened?)
* Have you met any British boys/girls yet? (Where did you meet them? What were they like?)
* Have you spoken on the phone to a British person? (Who did you speak to? Why did you speak to him/her?)
* Have you tried any new sports? (What was it/What were they?) Did you like it/them?

b Compare and discuss your answers in groups.

4 What has just happened?

a Work in teams (A and B). Look at the picture. Write down as many things as you can which have just happened.

Example:
The man on the pier has just caught a fish.

b Team A say one thing they have got on their list. If team B have also got it, they cross it out on their list. Then team B say one thing they have got on their list, and team A cross it out, etc. The team with the longest remaining correct list is the winner.

Grammar summary: page 85

1 Telephoning

Using public telephones

Read the instructions below and put them in the correct order.

- Put your money in.
- Dial the number you want.
- Pick up the receiver and listen for dialling tone.
- Don't forget to take your unused coins back.
- Have your money ready (10p, 50p, £1).
- Speak when somebody answers.

Using cardphones

Read the instructions. Match them with the pictures and fill in the blanks next to the pictures.

- Don't forget to take out your card.
- Buy a phonecard from a shop.
- Dial the number you want.
- Pick up the receiver and listen for the dialling tone.
- Put your phonecard in the slot.
- Speak when somebody answers.

1 ....

2 ....

3 ....

4 ....

5 ....

6 ....

How to make an International call

1 Dial 010.

2 Dial the code for your country.

Examples:
France 33   Italy 39   West Germany 49   Japan 81   Brazil 55

3 Now dial the code for the town/city you want *without* the first figure.

Examples:
Athens 1   Stockholm 8   Barcelona 3

4 Finally, dial the number of the person you want to speak to.

Now write down the full number of your own family or a friend in your country.

010	46	8	268557
international code	country code (Sweden)	city code (Stockholm)	number of family, friend, etc.

2 🖭 Cashing traveller's cheques

a Practise the conversation in pairs. A is the student, B is the bank clerk. Change roles.

b Now act out the conversation without looking in the book.

A *Can I cash these traveller's cheques, please?*
B *Yes, certainly. Have you got your passport, please?*
A *No, I'm afraid I haven't.*
B *Have you got any other means of identification?*
A *Yes, I've got my identity card.*
B *That's fine. Can you sign them there, please, and fill in the date. It's the 18th today . . . That's fine. How would you like the money? In fives or tens?*
A *In fives, please . . . Thanks very much.*

3 🖭 Changing money

A *Yes?*
B *I'd like to change these Italian lire into pounds, please.*
A *Certainly. That's 50,000 lire altogether in notes. But I'm afraid we can't change the coins.*
B *Oh, I see.*

A *Now, can you write your name and address on this form, please?*
B *My address in England or in Italy?*
A *Your address in England. Thank you. How would you like the money—in fives or tens?*
B *In tens, please. Thank you.*

Practise the dialogue in pairs. Change the underlined words if necessary. Change roles.

1 🎧 Sound right

a Listen to these pairs of words. What is the difference in pronunciation between them?

A	B
chip	cheap
pot	port

b Listen again and repeat the words.

c Now listen and write down which of the two sounds you hear. Write A or B in the boxes.

1 ☐☐☐☐
2 ☐☐☐☐

d Write down the eight words you hear. Each word you hear contains one of the sounds you've been practising.

1 ....
2 ....
3 ....
4 ....
5 ....
6 ....
7 ....
8 ....

2 Listen to this

What's wrong?

a 🎧 Form two teams. Listen carefully to the story on the cassette. How many mistakes can you hear? Make notes as you listen.

b Each team compare their notes and make a list of all the mistakes they heard. Which team found the most?

3 Work on words

Each of the words on the left is part of a word on the right.

Example:
A letter is part of a word.

1	A letter	a) a wall
2	A player	b) a bike
3	A screen	c) a club
4	A branch	d) a television
5	A brick	e) a boat
6	A finger	f) a classroom
7	A member	g) a word
8	A sail	h) a team
9	A blackboard	i) a house
10	A stomach	j) a light
11	An engine	k) a bath
12	A bulb	l) a body
13	A tap	m) a tree
14	A pedal	n) a hand
15	A handle	o) a sentence
16	A musician	p) a bird
17	A toe	q) a week
18	A flame	r) a foot
19	A wing	s) an orchestra
20	A soldier	t) a cup
21	A day	u) an army
22	A word	v) a fire
23	A roof	w) a car

4 Play games in English

Think of another

a Form two teams, A and B.

b The teacher chooses a word group, for example animals, things in the kitchen, a restaurant.

c Team A says a word related to the word group within 5 seconds.

d Team B says another word and so on until one team cannot think of a word or they say a word which does not belong to the group. The team who say the last correct word get an extra point. The teacher then chooses a new word group.

Example:
Teacher	*rooms*	
Team A	*kitchen*	(one point)
Team B	*bathroom*	(one point)
Team A	*bedroom*	(one point)
Team B	*hall*	(one point)

5 Read and think

Combine sentences from the two columns to make examples of British graffiti ('writing on walls').

Example:
Keep this bus tidy. Throw your tickets out of the window!

1 Keep this bus tidy.
2 Save water.
3 I'd enjoy the day more
4 Not long ago I could never finish anything.
5 Do you find it difficult to make up your mind?
6 Please don't write on these walls.
7 Nothing smells better than Brut after-shave.
8 I hate graffiti.
9 For the ten millionth time,
10 Women like the simple things in life.
11 If at first you don't succeed,
12 Always be sincere
13 Things are not as bad as they may seem.
14 Lisa, I love you, I need you, I'd go through fire for you, climb mountains for you, die for you!

a) Then use nothing.
b) I hate all Italian food.
c) Why? Do you want us to type?
d) See you on Saturday—if it isn't raining.
e) Bath with a friend!
f) stop exaggerating!!!
g) But now I...
h) No— they're much worse!
i) Like men!
j) give up!
k) Throw your tickets out of the window!
l) if it started later.
m) Well...er...yes...and...er ...no
n) even if you don't mean it.

6 Time to talk

a Look at the list and mark things you like doing with a tick (√).

b Mark things you don't like doing with a cross (X).

c Mark things you don't mind doing with a zero (0).

d Now compare your list with a partner's. Give reasons why you like or don't like doing different things.

e Put in order (1–3) the three things you most like doing and the three things you least like doing.

hearing the phone ring
visiting relatives
staying in bed on Saturday morning
losing a game or match.
being alone
going to bed at night.
washing my hair
having a bath
talking in front of a lot of people
repairing my bike/motorbike/car
getting a letter from a friend
washing up.

f Find out which are the three most popular things and the three most unpopular things among everybody in the class.

7 Now you're here

Ask a British person these questions and note down his/her answers.

1 Do you rent or own your television?
2 How much does a television licence cost?
3 Where does the money go?
4 Which TV channel do you watch most?
5 What's your favourite programme?
6 What's your least favourite programme?
7 Which is the most popular programme at the moment?
8 How many hours an evening do you watch television (on average)?
9 Do you think they show too much violence on television?
10 How often do they have advertisements on ITV?
11 What's the difference between:

   a game show/a chat show
   a soap opera/a situation comedy
   a current affairs programme/the news
   a play/a documentary?
12 What sort of programmes do they have
   on BBC | Radio 1?
           | Radio 2?
           | Radio 3?
           | Radio 4?
13 Which of the four stations do you listen to most?
14 Which one has the most listeners?
15 What commercial radio stations are there in this area?

Compare your answers in class.

UNIT SIX
LESSON ONE

What's in a name?

Did you know that:

- the most common surname in English is Smith. A 'smith' was a person who made things from metal. The same name translated is also very common in many European languages.

- in Britain, your first name is more important than your middle name. But in Germany, for example, the opposite is true.

- in English, you don't use the titles 'Mr', 'Mrs', and 'Miss' as often as in many other languages. So, for example, you cannot say Mr Peter or Miss Christine. In most languages you can address a stranger with the words 'Mr', 'Mrs' or 'Miss' (translated of course). This is not 'correct' English.

- nowadays it is becoming more and more common for girls and women to use the 'new' word 'Ms' (instead of Mrs or Miss).

- in 1989, the five most popular boys' names in Britain were: 1 Christopher, 2 Matthew, 3 David, 4 James, 5 Daniel. Forty years earlier, when the fathers of these boys were born, the five most popular names were: 1 David, 2 John, 3 Peter, 4 Michael, 5 Alan.

- in 1989, the five most popular girls' names were: 1 Sarah, 2 Claire, 3 Emma, 4 Laura, 5 Rebecca. In 1950, they were: 1 Susan, 2 Linda, 3 Christine, 4 Margaret, 5 Carol.

- the sexiest names, according to a British survey, are David and Susan.

- some of the most embarrassing surnames in Britain are Longbottom, Smelly, Death, Eatwell, and Rainwater.

- the most common first name in the world is Mohammed, and the most common surname is Chang? But nobody in the world has the name Mohammed Chang!

- black parents in Britain choose much more original names for their children than white parents. Some typical 'black' names are: Byron, Winston, Curtis, Ashley, Latoya, and Ebony.

1 Make true sentences

Match the name on the left with the rest of the sentence on the right.

Example: 1 – e

1 Mohammed			a) sexiest boy's name.
2 David			b) most common surname in English.
3 Sarah			c) newest way of addressing a woman.
4 Susan	is		d) most popular boy's name in 1989.
5 Chang		the	e) most common first name in the world.
6 Christopher	was		f) most popular girl's name in 1950.
7 Ms			g) most common surname in the world.
8 Smith			h) most popular girl's name in 1989.

2 Class survey

Work in groups. Ask each other questions to find out:

- if any students have got the same first name, middle name or surname
- who's got the longest surname
- who's got the shortest surname
- who's got the sexiest first name
- who's got a name which is common in other languages
- which first/surname is the most difficult to pronounce
- which first names in the class are from the Bible.

3 Ask each other

Work in pairs. Take it in turn to ask each other the questions below.

1 Which of the English names on page 36 do you like the best / least?
2 What is the most popular boy's / girl's name in your country now?
3 Do you like your first name? Would you like to change it?
4 Do your family call you by your first name or do they shorten it?
5 What's the most common surname in your country?
6 When people get married in your country, does the woman change her surname to that of her husband?
7 Do you have your mother's surname or your father's?
8 Are the same first names popular now as when your parents were young?

4 What's the answer?

Work in pairs. Student A reads the instructions below and student B reads the instructions on page 79.

Read the information about these four people.

- Sarah is younger than Laura.
- Daniel is older than Laura.
- Sarah is taller than Laura.
- Laura isn't as tall as Daniel.
- James isn't as heavy as Daniel.
- Laura is lighter than James.

Ask each other questions and find out:

who's the oldest
who's the youngest
who's the tallest
who's the shortest
who's the heaviest
who's the lightest.

Example:
A *Is James younger than Sarah?*
B *No, he isn't / Yes, he is. / I don't know.*

5 Crazy world records

🎧 Listen to the cassette and fill in the missing information.

The most hamburgers eaten:
. . . . . hamburgers and buns in
. . . . . minutes . . . . . seconds.
Birmingham, England. June . . . . .

The most ice-cream eaten:
. . . . . kilos in . . . . . seconds. England.
July . . . . .

The longest non-stop dancing record:
. . . . . hours. Montreal. September . . . . .

The biggest selling record:
'. . . . .' by Bob Geldof and Midge Ure for 'Live-aid' sold
. . . . . copies in . . . . .

The longest kiss:
. . . . . days . . . . . hours. Chicago. USA.
September . . . . .

6 What's wrong?

Work in pairs. Student A reads the statements which all have mistakes in them. Student B corrects the mistakes.

Example:
A *The name Claire is more popular than Sarah.*
B *No, the name Claire isn't as popular as the name Sarah.*

1 In Britain your middle name is more important than your first name.

2 In Germany your middle name isn't as important as your first name.
3 The name Matthew is more popular than Christopher.
4 The name James is not as popular as Daniel.
5 The name David is more popular now than it was in the 1950s.
6 The name James isn't as old as the name Alan.

7 Make comparisons

Work in pairs or groups. Compare Britain and your country. Use the words in the box if you want to.

Examples:
Prices are lower in Britain than in Germany.
The weather is not as hot as it is in Spain.
Television programmes are better in Britain than they are in Norway.

prices   clothes   the food   buses
the weather   police officers   boys
TV programmes   girls   the coffee
the language   drivers   bathrooms
houses   the traffic   gardens

Grammar summary: page 85

1 Clothes

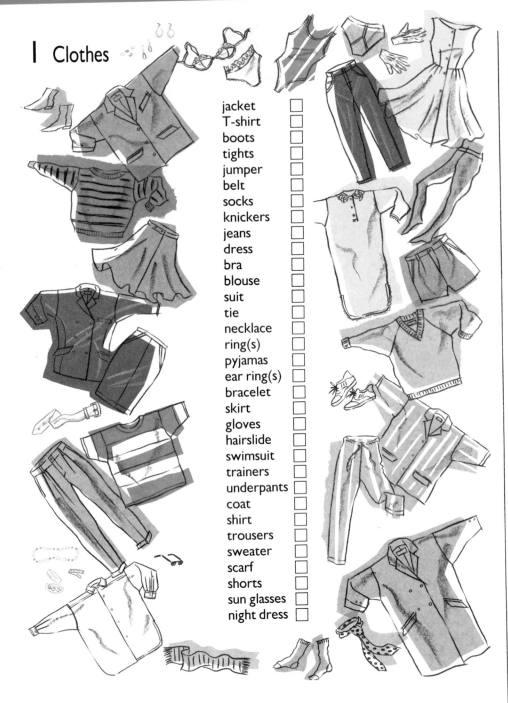

- jacket ☐
- T-shirt ☐
- boots ☐
- tights ☐
- jumper ☐
- belt ☐
- socks ☐
- knickers ☐
- jeans ☐
- dress ☐
- bra ☐
- blouse ☐
- suit ☐
- tie ☐
- necklace ☐
- ring(s) ☐
- pyjamas ☐
- ear ring(s) ☐
- bracelet ☐
- skirt ☐
- gloves ☐
- hairslide ☐
- swimsuit ☐
- trainers ☐
- underpants ☐
- coat ☐
- shirt ☐
- trousers ☐
- sweater ☐
- scarf ☐
- shorts ☐
- sun glasses ☐
- night dress ☐

a Put a symbol after each word like this:

- ☑ if you're wearing it *now*
- ⊘ if you're *not* wearing it now but you've got it in Britain
- ⊙ if you've got it at home in your country but *not* with you in Britain
- ☒ if you haven't got it or never wear it.

Compare your lists.

b Work in pairs. Make a list of the things which are not *usually* worn by both sexes.

2 🎧 Shopping for clothes

A Can I help you?
B No, thanks, I'm just looking.

(two minutes later)

B Excuse me. Have you got these trousers in my size?
A What size are you?
B I don't know in inches, I'm afraid. I'm 71 centimetres I think.
A 71. That's 28 inches. These are all 28 inch waist.

(later)

B Can I try these on, please?
A Yes, of course. The changing room's over there.

(later)

A They suit you.
B But I'm afraid they don't fit me. They're too small. Have you got a size bigger?
A Yes, these are 29 waist.

(later)

B Yes, these are fine. I'll have them, thanks. How much are they?
A They're £27.45 . . . Is that all?
B Yes, thanks. Can I pay for them with a traveller's cheque?
A Have you got your passport with you?
B Yes . . . here.
A Can you sign the cheque, please . . . Good, that's fine, thanks.

Practise the dialogue in pairs. Change roles. Use your own ideas if you want to.

Sizes

British shops are slowly changing over to the metric system (centimetres/metres instead of inches/feet/yards). Many department stores use both systems but most small clothes shops still use British measurements.

Shoes		Sweaters/Jumpers		Jeans/Trousers		Dresses		For T-shirts, tights, pyjamas, etc.
British	Continental	British	Continental	British	Continental	British	Continental	XS = extra small
4	36	32	42	24 in.	60 cm.	8	36	S = small
4½	37	34	44	26	65	10	38	M = medium
5	37½	36	46	28	70	12	40	L = large
5½	38-38½	38	48	30	75	14	42	XL = extra large
6	39	40	50	32	80	16	44	
6½	40			34	85	18	46	
7	40½-41							
8	42							
9	43							
9½	44							
10	45							

3 Act it out

a Work out your size in T-shirts/jeans or trousers/sweaters/shoes.

b Work in pairs. Imagine you want to buy the things in these pictures. Act out the dialogues. Use phrases like:

It's		big.
They're	too	small.
		long.
		short.
		tight.
		loose.
		expensive.

They're too big.

4 What do they buy?

Listen to the cassette and fill in the missing information in the table below.

	Item of clothing	Colour	Size	Cost
First customer				
Second customer				
Third customer				

5 Role play

Work in pairs. Student A reads the instructions below. Student B reads the instructions on page 79.

You want to buy a pair of jeans, size 28.

You like blue or black jeans. You only really want to spend £18.

Talk to the shop assistant. Ask him/her about colours, size, prices, etc. Don't leave the shop until you get what you want.

Use phrases like these:

Yes, I'm looking for . . .
I'm size . . .
Can I try them on, please?
Have you got a bigger/smaller size?
I'm afraid they're too . . .

Summary of English in situations

- buying clothes
- talking about sizes and colours

1 🎧 Sound right

a Listen to these pairs of words. What is the difference in pronunciation between them?

hot	hat
sock	sack
top	tap

b Listen again and repeat the words.

c Now listen to these pairs of words. What is the difference in pronunciation between them?

cat	cut
mad	mud
ran	run

d Listen again and repeat the words.

e Choose six of the words in a) or c) and write them in boxes like this:

hot	tap	mad
sack	run	cut

Listen to the teacher and cross out your words when you hear them. When all of your words are crossed out, shout 'Bingo'. The first person to call 'Bingo' is the winner (if all his/her words are correct).

2 Play games in English

Add a word

a Form two teams, A and B.

b The teams take it in turn to write words on the blackboard. The other team add a word which must lead to a *real* sentence.

Example:
Team A *Yesterday*
Team B *I*
Team A *saw*
Team B *my*
Team A *brother*
Team B *who*
Team A *has*
Team B *got*
Team A *a*
Team B *black*
Team A *car*   (one point)

c If one team cannot think of another word to add of if they add an incorrect word, or one that does not continue the sentence, the other team win a point.

3 🎧 Listen to this

a Listen to the radio news on the cassette. What are the 'stories' or items about? Put ticks [√] in the correct boxes below.

☐ politics
☐ information for motorists
☐ pop music
☐ world news
☐ weather
☐ the Royal Family
☐ sport
☐ crime

b Listen again and mark the following sentences true [√] or false [×].

1 The accident was at junction 10. ☐
2 The lorry driver was killed. ☐
3 Billy J. Bonds arrived by plane. ☐
4 His tour includes France and Germany. ☐
5 The police have found the escaped prisoner. ☐
6 He was in prison for murdering a railway guard. ☐
7 Liverpool won the match. ☐
8 69,000 people watched the game. ☐
9 Tonight will be wet and windy. ☐
10 The weather tomorrow will be the same. ☐

4 Work on words

Where's it going?

Choose the correct preposition of movement for each of the pictures.

away from	round	up	over	
across	into	along	down	
under	through	towards	off	
onto	out of			

1   2

3   4

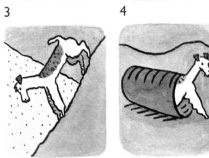
5   6

7   8

Now draw pictures for the other six prepositions.

5 Time to talk

a Read the questionnaire and mark your answers with a tick (√).

b Discuss your answers in groups.

c Find out what percentage of the class agreed or disagreed with each statement.

	I agree	I'm not sure	I don't agree
1 Boys should open doors for girls.	☐	☐	☐
2 Boys should be older than their girlfriends.	☐	☐	☐
3 Girls should be shorter than their boyfriends.	☐	☐	☐
4 Girls should not 'chat up' boys.	☐	☐	☐
5 It's embarrassing if a girl asks a boy to dance.	☐	☐	☐
6 Boys should always pay for their girlfriends.	☐	☐	☐
7 It's normal for boys to want several girlfriends.	☐	☐	☐
8 Women should keep their own surnames when they get married.	☐	☐	☐

6 Read and think

Read the two stories. The lines in them have been mixed up. Put them in the correct order so the stories make sense.

☐ **Farmer** *What do you want?*

☐ **Salesman** *It's so clever, so powerful, that it can do half the work on your farm.*

☐ **Farmer** *What can it do?*

☐ **Salesman** *Good afternoon, Mr Giles. Have you got a moment?*

☐ **Farmer** *In that case, I'll have two of them.*

☐ **Salesman** *I'd just like to tell you about our new SuperDuper tractor.*

☐ **Woman** *I think you've made a mistake.*

☐ **Piano tuner** *Good afternoon, madam. I've come to tune your piano.*

☐ **Piano tuner** *You mean you haven't got a piano?*

☐ **Woman** *Yes – what do you want?*

☐ **Piano tuner** *No, madam. You haven't. But your neighbours have.*

☐ **Woman** *No, we've got a piano. But I haven't asked anyone to come and tune it.*

7 Now you're here

a Ask a British person these questions.

1 How many hours do you work a week?
2 How many weeks' holiday do you get a year?
3 If you won the pools, would you give up work?
4 How much time do you spend:
watching television?
reading?
on DIY?
5 How often do you go out in the evening?
6 How often do you go to:
the cinema?
the theatre?
a pub?
church?
a restaurant?
a disco?
7 What are your interests/hobbies?
8 Are you a member of any clubs/ societies?
9 How often do you get some form of exercise (e.g. jogging, squash)?
10 Where do you usually go on holiday?
11 How long do you go for?
12 When do you usually go?
13 How do you get there?
14 Where do you stay (in a hotel/on a camping site/in a caravan, etc.)?
15 What do you do when you're on holiday?
16 Which foreign countries have you visited?
17 Which ones would you like to go back to?
18 Which countries would you like to visit? Why?

b Tell other students your most interesting answers.

GRAMMAR IN ACTION

How wrong can you be?

Are 'experts' always right? Read the following, and decide for yourself!

"You won't succeed in this business if you sing like that. Why don't you go back to driving a truck?"
Jim Denny, a Memphis manager, to Elvis Presley after his first concert, in 1954.

"The big question today is: 'How long will Rock 'n' Roll last?' We don't think it will last long at all."
Cashbox, an American music magazine, 1955.

"You'll be all right if you learn to be a secretary, or get married, but you'll never act in movies."
Advice to Marilyn Monroe from a Hollywood film producer in 1944.

"The telephone's an amazing invention, but who will ever want to use one?"
Rutherford B. Hayes, President of the United States, 1876.

"Television won't become important in your lifetime or mine."
The Editor of the BBC magazine, *The Listener*, in 1936.

"Man will not fly for fifty years."
Wilbur Wright, in 1901. Only two years later, in 1903, he became, with his brother Orville, the first man to fly.

"There will never be a woman Prime Minister in my lifetime."
Margaret Thatcher, speaking in 1976.

"Man will never be able to reach the moon, even if he tries for a thousand years."
Dr Lee de Forest, famous American inventor, 1957.

"This ship will never sink."
One of the designers of The Titanic, a short time before it sank, in 1912.

"This war (World War I), the greatest of all wars, is not just another war. It will be the last war."
H.G. Wells, English writer and historian, 1914.

"I think there will be a world market for about five computers."
Thomas J. Watson, Chairman of IBM, 1943.

Who said what?

Match the sentences below with the people who might have said them.

) Wilbur Wright
) Dr Lee de Forest
) Rutherford B. Hayes
) H. G. Wells
) Jim Denny
• the Hollywood producer
) a designer of The Titanic
) *Cashbox* magazine
• the Editor of *The Listener*
• Thomas J. Watson

1 You're the right shape, I guess, but you'll never be an actress.
2 People are quite happy just to listen – who needs pictures?
3 After this, no country will be stupid enough to start another one.
4 We think that people will soon get tired of this kind of music.
5 You look good and you move OK but that voice . . . !
6 Even if we try for a thousand years we won't be able to do it.
7 My brother and I are both working hard on it but we're still a long way from solving all the problems.
8 We'd like to sell more, of course, but they're so big and expensive!
9 Even if it hits something it'll be all right.
10 I think people will always prefer to write a letter.

2 What will happen if . . . ?

Listen to these situations. When the teacher stops the tape say what you think *will happen*. There is an example first.

3 Message in a bottle

Work in groups. You are on a ship which is sinking fast. You can swim to a nearby desert island. The island is small (1,000 square metres) with no fresh water or animal life. There are a few trees. The nearest inhabited island is several hundred miles away.

a You have ten minutes to agree which five objects you will take with you to the island. Remember that you probably won't be rescued for several months. Try to say how you will use the things that you take from the sinking ship. Also say why you *won't* take other things.

Examples:
We'll use the X to make food.
We won't take Y because . . .
We'll make a fire with . . .

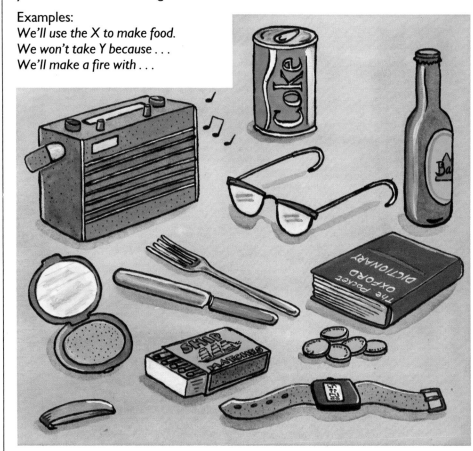

b Explain to the other groups which objects you will take and why.

c Now answer the following questions. (You cannot change your mind about the objects you will take.)

1 How will you drink? (Remember you can't drink sea water.)
2 How will you make a fire?
3 How will you get food?
4 How will you cook?
5 How will you collect water?
6 How will you keep warm and dry at night?
7 How will you attract the attention of passing ships?
8 How will you pass the time?

Grammar summary: page 86

43

1 Telephoning – telephone numbers

A What's your telephone number, Jessica?
B Two–double three–four–oh–nine.
A Hang on, I'll write it down . . .
   What does 'double three' mean?
B Three–three.
A And what about 'oh'?
B That means 'zero', of course.
A So . . . two, double three, four, oh, nine.
B That's right.

2 What are their numbers?

Listen to these short conversations and write down the telephone numbers you hear.

1 ....
2 ....
3 ....
4 ....
5 ....

3 Quick questions

Go round the class and ask each other, 'What's your telephone number?' Write down students' names and numbers. The winner is the student with the most correct telephone numbers after three minutes. You can give your telephone number in Britain or in your country.

4 Speaking on the phone

A Hello. 387 200.
B Hello. Could I speak to Clare, please?
A Speaking.
B Oh, I didn't recognize your voice. This is Carlos.
A Oh hello, Carlos. How are you?

Practise this dialogue in pairs, using your own names and telephone numbers. Change roles.

5 Telephone messages

A 446 3720.
B Hello. Could I speak to Peter, please?
A No, I'm sorry, he's out at the moment. Can I take a message?
B Yes, please. Could you ask him to phone me when he gets in, please?
A Yes, of course. Who's that speaking?
B This is Marta.
A All right, Marta. I'll tell him as soon as he gets in. Does he know your number?
B I'm not sure. Anyway, it's 623379.
A Just a moment. 622379?
B No, 623379.
A All right, Marta, I've got that now.
B Thanks very much. Goodbye.
A Bye.

Practise the dialogue in pairs using your own names and telephone numbers.

6 Take the messages

Listen to the telephone conversations on the cassette. Fill in the gaps in the messages.

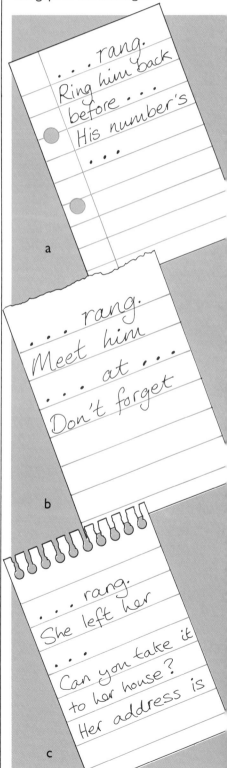

. . . rang.
Ring him back
before . . .
His number's
. . .

a

. . . rang.
Meet him
at . . .
. . .
Don't forget

b

. . . rang.
She left her
. . .
Can you take it
to her house?
Her address is

c

44

7 Leave a message

a Form groups of five or six students and sit in a line. The first student in the line (A) writes a telephone message. The message should include:

- his/her name
- the time and place that A wants to meet X (the last person in the line)
- what X should bring, e.g. a cassette player, a friend, etc.

b Student A 'rings' the next student in the line (B), and whispers the message to him/her. Student B then whispers the message to the next student (C), etc.

c The student at the end of the line (X) writes down the message. Students A and X then compare their messages. Are they the same?

Example:
Francesca rang. She wants you to meet her outside the sports centre at 7.30. She wants you to bring your squash racket and a ball.

8 🖭 Days and dates

a Write down the dates which you hear mentioned in the short conversations on the cassette.

Example:
23.10.67

1 ....
2 ....
3 ....
4 ....

b Where do the conversations take place?

Note: You *write* 23rd April 1989 or 23/4/89. You *say* the twenty-third of April, nineteen eighty-nine.

9 A quiz

a Form two teams. Ask each other these questions:

- What is the day after Wednesday?
- What is the day before Wednesday?
- What is the day between Saturday and Monday?
- If it's Thursday today:
  a) what day is it tomorrow?
  b) what day was it yesterday?
- What's the day after tomorrow?
- What was the day before yesterday?
- In which day is the third letter D?
- What's the third month of the year?
- What's the tenth month of the year?
- Which month comes between September and July?
- In which month is the third letter C?
- In which month is the last letter L?
- In which month is the second letter O?
- Which is the shortest month of the year?
- Which month has the longest day?
- Which month has the shortest name?
- Which month has the longest name?
- Which three months begin with the same letter?

b Make up more questions, like those above. Ask the other team your questions.

10 Whose birthday?

a Each student writes out the date of his/her birthday on two pieces of paper.

Example:

b Students then give the pieces of paper to the teacher. The teacher puts them all in a bag or box.

c The teacher gives each student two pieces of paper, with *different* dates on. (They must not get their own birthday.)

d Students then go round the class asking each other, 'When's your birthday?'

The winner is the first student to find the two people who have got his/her birthday on their pieces of paper.

Summary of English in situations

- using the telephone
- telephone numbers
- taking messages on the telephone
- talking about days and dates

1 ▦ Sound right

a Listen to these pairs of words. What is the difference in pronunciation between them?

buy	bay
guy	gay
high	hay

b Listen again and repeat the words.

c Now listen to these pairs of words. What is the difference in prounuciation between them?

saw	so
or	oh
walk	woke

d Listen again and repeat the words.

e Choose six of the words in a) and c) and write them in boxes like this:

hay	so	buy
or	guy	woke

Listen to the teacher and cross out your words when you hear them. When all of your words are crossed out, shout 'Bingo'. The first person to call 'Bingo' is the winner (if all his/her words are correct).

2 Listen to this

▦ Listen to part of a television game show. Write down your answers.

1 ....

2 ....

3 ....

4 ....

5 ....

3 Work on words

a Think of a word which connects each of the four words.

Example:

typewriter/secretary/word processor/telephone = `o` `f` `f` `i` `c` `e`

b Add other words to each word group.

1 waiter/menu/tip/bill = ☐☐☐☐☐☐☐☐☐

2 mattress/sheet/dream/pillow = ☐☐☐

3 dial/receiver/code/answer = ☐☐☐☐☐☐☐☐

4 fog/showers/cloudy/fine = ☐☐☐☐☐☐☐

5 lawn/flowerbed/hedge/path = ☐☐☐☐☐☐

6 company/profit/product/invest = ☐☐☐☐☐☐☐☐

7 blonde/wig/curly/cut = ☐☐☐☐

8 goal/kick/score/penalty = ☐☐☐☐☐☐☐

9 bytes/program/keyboard/screen = ☐☐☐☐☐☐☐☐

10 hotel/beach/flight/sight-seeing = ☐☐☐☐☐☐☐

11 moon/sleep/dark/black = ☐☐☐☐☐

12 toast/coffee/cereals/marmalade = ☐☐☐☐☐☐☐☐☐

4 Play games in English

First and last

a Form two teams, A and B.

b The teacher gives team A the middle of a word.

Example: *ONT*

Team A have to make a word by adding *one* letter before and after 'ONT'.

There is a time limit of 15 seconds.

Example: *M–ONT–H*

c The teacher then gives Team B the middle of a word, etc.

d If after 15 seconds a team cannot think of a word or make a mistake, the other team have a chance to make the word. You get one point for each correct word.

5 Time to talk

a In pairs or groups, try to work out the answers to these problems. You can ask the teacher as many questions as you want but he/she can only answer 'yes' or 'no'.

b If you think you know the right answer, don't shout it out. Write it down on a piece of paper and show it to the teacher. He/She will tell you if it is the right answer or not.

1 The King was dying and he called his two sons to his bed. The King and his sons loved horse racing and the King had a strange sense of humour. He said: 'I'll give my crown and my kingdom to the son whose horse loses a 20 kilometre race!'

The following day the two sons started the race trying to ride as slowly as possible. After six hours they had travelled one kilometre and they were still together. They stopped to have a drink in a river and suddenly one of the sons said, 'I've got a good idea!' A few moments later they continued the race riding as fast as they could. Why?

2 A man found a dead body in the middle of a field. Next to the body was an unopened package. He immediately knew how the person had died. How?

3 Mr Ford lives on the twelfth floor of a block of flats. Every day he takes the lift down to the street, catches the bus and goes to work.

In the evening he comes home from work. If he is alone when he enters the building, he takes the lift to the sixth floor and then walks the rest of the way to the twelfth floor. If there is somebody else with him he takes the lift all the way to the twelfth floor. Why?

6 Read and think

Look at the diagram and then follow the instructions below.

+ = add
− = subtract
× = multiply
÷ = divide

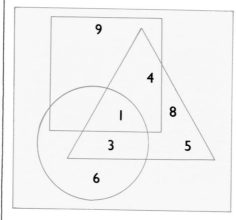

a Add together all the numbers which are in the triangle but *not* in the square.

b Subtract that number from the sum of all the numbers which are in the triangle but *not* in the circle.

c Multiply that number by the number which is in the square but *not* in the triangle or circle.

d Divide that number by the number which is in the square, the circle and the triangle.

What is the answer?

7 Now you're here

a Ask a British adult:

1 What kind of school(s) did you go to?
2 How old were you when you left?
3 Was your school co-educational?
4 Did you wear a uniform?
5 Did you enjoy school (Why/Why not)?
6 Did the school have corporal punishment?
7 What did you call your teachers (e.g. Sir, Miss)?

b Ask a British student:

1 What kind of school do you go to?
2 Is it co-educational?
3 Do you have to wear a uniform?
4 What school rules are there?
5 Do you call your teachers by their first names?
6 What happens if you break school rules?
7 Where do you have lunch?
8 Which sports do you play at school?
9 What subjects are you studying?
10 How much homework do you get?
11 How often do you have exams?
12 What exam are you working for now?
13 How long is your Christmas/Easter/summer holiday?
14 When are you going to leave school?
15 What sort of activities/clubs are there at your school?
16 Do students normally go to the university in their home town or do they go away to university?
17 What are the good things about your school?
18 What are the bad things about your school?

Pet hates

'I don't mind people taking photographs of me. But I hate smiling for a photograph when the flash doesn't work. (The next time, of course, it works. But instead of smiling I'm blinking!)'

'I can't stand people who look at themselves in shop windows as they walk past.'

'I don't like getting on a train or bus and sitting down on a seat which is still warm.'

'I can't stand finding pieces of other people's toast, or marmalade, in the butter.'

'I don't like using pencils or pens which have teethmarks in them.'

'I can't stand going to the cinema with someone who has seen the film before—they can't help telling you what's going to happen next.'

'It really annoys me when there's just one piece of pizza or cake left, which I want—but I can't have it because I'm afraid of looking greedy.'

I Make complete sentences

a Match each verb in brackets with the rest of the sentence on the right.

b Now use one of the expressions on the left to make a complete sentence.

Example:
I don't like smiling for a photograph.

I hate	1 (smile)	a) pencils with teeth marks.
	2 (go)	b) for a photograph.
I don't like	3 (sit)	c) to the cinema with a person who's seen the film before.
	4 (find)	
I can't stand	5 (use)	d) greedy if I want the last piece of pizza.
	6 (look)	e) down on a seat which is still warm.
		f) pieces of toast in the butter.

2 Why are they angry?

Say why the people are angry and write a sentence under each picture. Use *can't stand, don't like* or *hate*.

1 *He hates going to the dentist's.*

2 ....

3 ....

4 ....

5 ....

6 ....

3 What makes you angry?

a Work in groups. Make a list of the things which make *you* angry. You can include examples from page 48 and Exercise 2 if you want.

b Make a list on the board of 'pet hates'. Is there anything on the list which *you* don't mind doing? Is there anything which *you* like doing?

4 Ask a British person

a Interview a British person about his/her 'pet hates'.

b Compare your answers in class. What makes British people angry most?

5 Ask and answer

Work in pairs. Make complete questions and then answer them.

1 Do you enjoy (go) to the cinema?
2 Do you like people (take) your photograph?
3 Are you good at (take) photographs?
4 Do you mind (find) pieces of other people's toast in the butter?
5 Do you go on (talk) if somebody is waiting to use the phone?
6 Before (sit) down on a bus or train, do you check to see if the seat is still warm?
7 What are you most afraid of (do)?
8 Can you stop yourself (tell) everybody what's going to happen if you've seen a film before?
9 Do you look at yourself in shop windows instead of (look) at the clothes, etc?
10 What are you looking forward to (do) when you get back to your country?

6 What's the word?

a 🎦 Form two teams. Listen to the cassette and take it in turns to answer the questions. Discuss your answers before answering. You get one point for a correct answer.

b Now write questions to ask the other team, like those you heard on the tape. Write five questions about people and five questions about things.

Example:
What do you call a person who . . . ?
What do you call a/the thing which you use to . . . ?

c Take it in turns to ask your questions. You get one point for a correct answer.

Grammar summary: page 86

49

1   Travelling by train

A   *Can I have a ticket to Oxford, please?*
B   *Single or return?*
A   *Return, please.*
B   *Are you coming back today?*
A   *Oh yes, this evening.*
B   *So you want a cheap day return then. That's £12.15 . . . Thank you.*
A   *What time does the next train leave, please?*
B   *At 10.37.*
A   *And what time does it get to Oxford?*
B   *At 12.08.*
A   *Which platform does it go from?*
B   *Platform 6.*
A   *Do I have to change?*
B   *Yes, change at Didcot.*
A   *Thanks very much.*

a   Practise the dialogue in pairs.

b   Change roles. Change the underlined words/numbers.

Example:

Chester	London
£15.60	£5.99
11.43	8.28
13.33	9.17
5	2
Crewe	Gravesend

2   How to get there

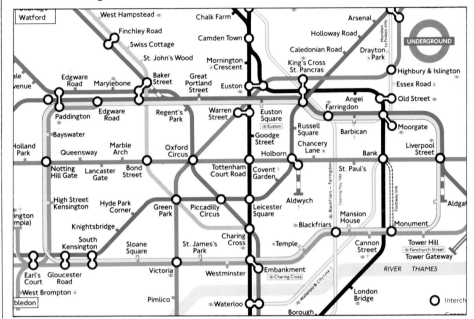

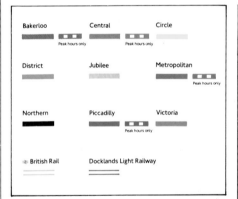

Look at the map of the Underground. In pairs work out the best way to do the following journeys:

- from Oxford Circus to Westminster
- from Piccadilly Circus to High Street Kensington
- from Victoria to St Paul's
- from Hyde Park Corner to Charing Cross
- from Marble Arch to Barbican.

Example:
from Covent Garden to Sloane Square

1   *Take the Piccadilly line, westbound.*
2   *Get off at South Kensington.*
3   *Change to the Circle line or the District line, eastbound.*
4   *Get off at Sloane Square.*

3   Travelling by bus

A   *Does this bus go to Oxford Circus, please?*
B   *Oxford Circus? No, you want the 74. There's one every six minutes.*

    (ten minutes later)

C   *Hold very tight now . . . Fares, please.*
A   *Oxford Circus, please.*
C   *65p.*
A   *Thanks. And can you tell me where to get off?*
C   *Oxford Circus? Right. Fares, please. Any more fares?*

Work in pairs. Change the underlined words to other places in London and other fares. Change roles.

4 🎧 Travelling by taxi

A Access Taxis.
B Can you send a taxi to 78, Queens Road, please?
A What's your name, please?
B Federica Pisani.
A Can you spell that?
B P–I–S–A–N–I.
A And where do you want to go?
B To the Odeon Cinema.
A Right, it'll be there in about ten minutes.
B Good. Thank you.

(10 minutes later)

A Taxi for Pisani.
B Yes, that's me. I'm coming.
A To the coach station, isn't it?
B No, to the Odeon Cinema, please.

(15 minutes later)

A Here we are.
B How much is that?
A £4.25.
B Thank you. Keep the change.

Practise the dialogue in pairs. Use your own names and addresses. Change roles.

5 Travelling by coach

Coaches are long-distance buses. They travel between all the big cities in Britain. They are quite fast, comfortable and cheap. Many coaches have toilets, and staff who serve drinks and snacks.

Work in pairs. Student A reads the instructions below. Student B reads the instructions on page 80.

You want to go to Bath. Ask student B questions to get the information you need. He/She will ask you for information about a trip to Brighton.

	To Bath	To Brighton
1 Cost of a day return ticket	...	£14.70
2 Time of the first coach you can catch	...	7.15
3 Time the coach arrives	...	11.15
4 Bay	...	2
5 Time of the last coach back	...	20.30

6 What's missing?

🎧 Listen to the short telephone conversations on the cassette and fill in the missing information in the table.

	Taxi company	Taxi to	Name of passenger	Address	Telephone number
1					
2					
3					

Summary of English in situations
• using public transport

1 🎧 Sound right

a How do you pronounce these words?

hot	history
half	happy
hand	hair
help	how
house	horse

b Listen and repeat the words on the cassette.

c Now listen and the repeat the pairs of words on the cassette.

d Now write down the words you hear on the cassette.

1 ....

2 ....

3 ....

4 ....

5 ....

6 ....

e Try and say these:

A high hill.
It's a horrible house.
How's your headache?
He had half a hamburger.
He hid his head in his hands.
He hit his hand with a heavy hammer.
Harriet and her husband had a holiday in Hawaii.

f Now listen and repeat the same phrases / sentences.

2 Listen to this

Expert witness?

a Look carefully at the picture of a robbery.

b 🎧 Now listen to the interview between a police officer and a witness. Work in groups. Make a list of the ten mistakes the witness makes.

3 Work on words

Find a word on the right which means the same, or nearly the same, as each word on the left.

Example: start   begin

1	start	a)	certain
2	closed	b)	last
3	repair	c)	probable
4	reply	d)	tidy
5	finish	e)	right
6	hard	f)	too
7	try	g)	awful
8	final	h)	begin
9	usually	i)	short
10	help	j)	mend
11	allow	k)	unusual
12	nearly	l)	shut
13	also	m)	find out
14	perhaps	n)	marvellous
15	cross	o)	ill
16	discover	p)	assist
17	leave	q)	answer
18	brief	r)	depart
19	terrible	s)	difficult
20	neat	t)	let
21	fantastic	u)	attempt
22	sick	v)	end
23	correct	w)	annoyed
24	likely	x)	maybe
25	definite	y)	almost
26	strange	z)	normally

4 Time to talk

a Tick (√) the jobs which each person does in your family at home and in the family you are staying with here.

	At home in your country			Here in Britain		
	You	Your mother	Your father	You	The man	The woman
Shopping						
Cooking						
Laying the table						
Clearing the table						
Washing the dishes						
Drying the dishes						
Ironing						
Hoovering						

b In groups discuss your answers. Who do you think should do these jobs?

5 Play games in English

Rhyming tennis

a Form two teams, A and B.

b Team A 'serves' by saying a word of one syllable.

c Team B must reply with another word of one syllable which rhymes with the first one. Team A replies with another word and so on.

Example: A *short*
      B *caught*
      A *bought*
      B *sort*

d The teacher checks that the teams know how to spell their words and that they know what they mean.

e When one team cannot think of another word (after a time limit of 5 seconds) the other team win the point. The winning team chooses the next word.

6 Read and think

You have only got *five* minutes to finish this exercise. Read all the instructions first.

1 Write your full name in the middle of a piece of paper.
2 Circle your surname.
3 Draw three small squares under your first name.
4 Write your date of birth (day, month, year) in the three boxes.
5 Draw a line below the *year* you were born.
6 Draw a line above the *month* you were born.
7 Draw a triangle in the top left-hand corner of the page.
8 Write exactly how old you are now (years, months, days) in the triangle.
9 In the bottom right-hand corner of the page write the second and third letters of the town/city where you are now.
10 In the top right-hand corner write the time it is now (in words).
11 If you're a boy, draw a vertical line through the middle of the page. If you're a girl, draw a horizontal line through the middle of the page.
12 Do not follow any of these instructions except the first one but do not say anything.

7 Now you're here

How do you say the following? Ask a British person if you're not sure.

1 It's 8.55 – we're late!
2 The train leaves at 15.35.
3 I was born on May 21st 1958.
4 Her telephone number's 0272 290033.
5 He's 1.70m tall.
6 It's 81°F today which is about 28°C.
7 The temperature's – 5°C.
8 The speed limit's 30 mph (about 50kph).
9 Queen Elizabeth I: 1558 – 1603.
10 They got a pay rise of 6.8%.
11 Between ⅔ and ¾ of British people have never been abroad.
12 The room was 78m².
13 $2H_2 + O_2 = 2H_2O$.
14 At the moment £1 = $1.86.
15 There are 2.5 million people unemployed.
16 I'm 5ft 6in.
17 The final score was Liverpool 3, Manchester United 0.
18 He won the 1500m.
19 The distance from London to New York is 5,506km.
20 $132 \div 12 \times 2 + 2 - 4 = 20$.
21 Mark your answers with a √ or a X.
22 She won £1,568,432 on the football pools.

UNIT NINE

LESSON ONE

Different countries, different times

An English language school in Brighton wanted its students to find out when or at what time things happen in Britain.

German boy What time do people start work in Britain? At eight o'clock?

English woman Oh no, I don't think so. I suppose factories start at eight thirty, but offices don't start till nine or nine thirty. We aren't very hard-working, are we?

German boy But work isn't everything, is it?

English woman No, I suppose not.

Spanish boy The shops in Britain close very early, don't they?

English boy Yes, I suppose so. They're open later in Spain, aren't they?

Spanish boy Yes, they stay open till eight or eight thirty. (pause) What time do your family eat in the evening?

English boy Oh, at about six o'clock.

Spanish boy You're not really hungry then, are you?

English boy Yes, I am.

Spanish boy Six o'clock's too early for me. In Spain we don't eat till ten.

English boy Well, you could ask your English family to eat later, couldn't you?

Spanish boy No, I don't think so – I'm only a guest . . . What time do you usually go to bed?

English boy My parents tell me to go to bed at eleven when they go up, but I usually watch TV till midnight.

Spanish boy It's strange that pubs shut at eleven, isn't it? That's the time they open in Spain!

Swedish girl You don't start school very early in the morning, do you?

English girl Yes, we do. We start at nine o'clock – that's early, isn't it?

Swedish girl No, not really. In Sweden we start at eight o'clock . . . You haven't started your summer holidays yet, have you?

English girl No, we haven't. They don't start until the last week in July.

Swedish girl But the summer's almost over then, isn't it?

English girl Yes, I'm afraid so . . .

1 Right or wrong?

Work in pairs. Student A reads sentences 1–4 and student B agrees or disagrees with them by saying, 'Yes, they do./No, they don't.' etc. Change roles.

☐ 1 Swedish pupils start school earlier than English pupils, don't they?

☐ 2 English pupils don't go to school in July, do they?

☐ 3 In Britain factory workers start earlier than office workers, don't they?

☐ 4 Shops in Britain don't close as late as shops in Spain, do they?

☐ 5 The English boy isn't hungry at six o'clock, is he?

☐ 6 Six o'clock is too early for the Spanish boy to eat, isn't it?

☐ 7 The English boy goes to bed at eleven o'clock, doesn't he?

☐ 8 The pubs don't close at eleven o'clock in Spain, do they?

2 What time . . . ?

🔲 Listen to the interviews on the cassette and fill in the missing information.

	Nationality	School summer holiday begins	School begins in morning	School ends	Shops close	Evening meal
1						
2						
3						

3 What's missing?

a Fill in the missing 'question tags'.

b Imagine the boy's answers.

c Practise the dialogue in pairs.

Girl *You aren't English, . . . ?*
Boy *. . .*
Girl *You speak good English, . . . ?*
Boy *. . .*
Girl *I've seen you here before, . . . ?*
Boy *. . .*
Girl *You come here often, . . . ?*
Boy *. . .*
Girl *You were here last night, . . . ?*
Boy *. . .*
Girl *You danced with one of my friends, . . . ?*
Boy *. . .*
Girl *You haven't told me your name yet, . . . ?*
Boy *. . .*
Girl *That's a funny name, . . . ?*
Boy *. . .*
Girl *You're a bit shy. . . . ?*
Boy *. . .*
Girl *You don't say much, . . . ?*
Boy *. . .*

4 Find out

a Work in pairs. If your partner is living with a British family, ask him/her what time they: get up/leave for work/have lunch/have their evening meal/go to bed.

b In his/her country,

what time do | people start work?
| schools start in the morning?
| schools finish in the evening?
| shops open/close?
| people have their evening meal?
| people go to bed?

When do schools start/finish their summer holidays?

5 Answer the questions

🔲 Answer the questions you hear on the cassette using one of the expressions below.

Yes, | *I think so.*
| *I hope so.*
| *I suppose so.*
| *I'm afraid so.*

No, | *I don't think so.*
| *I hope not.*
| *I suppose not.*
| *I'm afraid not.*

6 What's happening?

Complete the sentences below to explain what's happening in each picture.

a) He's asking ....

b) He's telling ....

c) He's asking ....

d) They want ....

Grammar summary: page 86

55

1 ☷ Asking permission

A Is it all right if I bring some friends home with me tonight?
B How many friends?
A Oh, I don't know, three or four.
B Or five or six . . .
A No, not that many.
B Yes, all right then.
A And is it OK if I give them something to eat?
B You mean a piece of toast or something—yes, of course.
A No, I meant, can I cook them something?
B Well, that depends what it is.
A Oh, only something very simple, like spaghetti.
B Yes, all right then.
A And may we play a few records—you know, to dance to?
B Now wait a minute! What time is all this going to happen?
A Oh, not very late.
B How late?
A Well, after the party at school.
B No, I'm sorry, we've got to go to work in the morning. How can we sleep if there's an all-night party going on down here?
A Oh, but I thought . . .

a Practise this dialogue in pairs. Change roles.

b Now write dialogues for the situations below. Use these phrases:

Is it all right if I . . . ?	Yes, of course.
Is it OK if I . . . ?	Yes, all right.
Can I . . . ?	Yes, sure.
Could I . . . ?	
May I . . . ?	No, I'm sorry (+ excuse)
	No, I'm afraid (+ excuse)

Example:
A Can I use the telephone, please?
B No, I'm sorry, I'm waiting for a call.

1

2

3

4

2 Invitations and offers

A Do you want to dance?
B Yes, OK.

A Would you like to sit down?
B Yes, good idea.

A Would you like a drink?
B Yes, please.

a Practise the dialogue in pairs.

b Student A invites B, using the words below.

Example: walk
A Would you like to go for a walk?
B Yes, OK. / Good idea!

walk	tennis
cinema	cup of coffee
disco	shopping
beach	drink
McDonald's	pizza

c Change roles.

3 Invitations and excuses

Listen to the conversation between Steve and Louise. What does she invite him to do? What excuses does he make?

	Louise's invitation	Steve's excuse
This evening		
Tomorrow evening		
Friday evening		
Saturday evening		

4 Making excuses

Work in pairs. Student A wants to go out with student B, but B doesn't want to go out with A. B makes excuses using the pictures below or his/her own ideas.

Example:

A *Would you like to come out tonight?*
B *No, I'm sorry. I've got a headache.*
A *What about tomorrow then?*

Start your excuses with phrases like:

No, I'm sorry, I'm . . . ing
No, I'm afraid I | must . . .
| 've got to . . .
| promised to . . .

2

3

4

5 Role play

Work in pairs. Student A reads the information below. Student B reads the information on page 80.

Situation 1

You want to go to a party with student B. You'll know most of the people at the party but B won't. It starts at about 9 o'clock and goes on till late. Phone B and invite him/her. Try to persuade him/her to come with you.

You can use phrases like these:

Let's . . .
Why don't we . . .
Why don't you want to?
Oh, come on!
Are you sure?

Situation 2
Student B phones you and invites you to go to the beach for a swim. You can't swim, you hate cold water and you haven't got a swimsuit. Make excuses but be friendly.

Summary of English in situations
● asking permission ● inviting and making offers ● accepting/refusing invitations and offers ● apologizing and making excuses

1 🔲 Sound right

a Listen to these words and mark the stressed syllables.

Example: problem

photograph	nowadays
people	important
favourite	address
marmalade	umbrella
butter	cinema
about	telephone
station	possible

b Listen again and circle the unstressed syllables with the sound [ə] in them.

Example: problem

c Listen again and repeat the words in a).

d Try to pronounce these words. There is only one stressed syllable in each word and the sound [ə] is in all of them.

afraid	passenger	happen
machine	escalator	woman
arrive	pronounce	London
doctor		

e Listen to the cassette and check your pronunciation.

2 Time to talk

Spot the differences

Work in pairs. Student A reads the instructions below. Student B reads the instructions on page 80.

Look at the picture below. Student B has a similar picture but with six differences. Describe your picture to Student B. Student B will describe his/her picture to you. Try to find the six differences.

3 Work on words

What do you say to a person who is:

1 talking too much?
2 still asleep at 11 am?
3 looking unhappy?
4 driving too fast?
5 getting very angry or excited?
6 going to walk in front of a bus?
7 annoying you?
8 knocking at your door?
9 leaving without waiting for you?
10 being very slow?
11 not sure about going somewhere with you?
12 speaking too quietly?

Choose from the phrases in the box.

Cheer up!	Shut up!	Hurry up!
Wake up!	Sit down!	Get out!
Come on!	Go away!	Come in!
Calm down!	Speak up!	Hang on!
Slow down!	Look out!	

4 Play games in English

Word nets

a Form two to four groups.

b In 3 minutes, each group thinks of six words which are associated with the word in the box. One member of the team writes each of the words in a 'word net' on a big piece of paper.

Example:

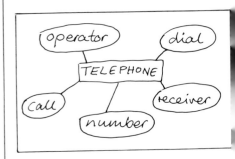

c Do the same with these words:

bread	winter	red
moon	grass	night

5 🎧 Listen to this

Listen to the voices on the cassette and write down a) who they are talking to and b) who they are.

1 a) ....
  b) ....

2 a) ....
  b) ....

3 a) ....
  b) ....

4 a) ....
  b) ....

5 a) ....
  b) ....

6 a) ....
  b) ....

7 a) ....
  b) ....

8 a) ....
  b) ....

9 a) ....
  b) ....

6 Read and think

Doctor, Doctor . . .

Read the jokes and choose the correct line from the sentences in the box below.

1 **Doctor:** Breathe in and out three times.
  Patient: Are you checking my lungs?
  Doctor: ....

2 **Woman:** I've got a serious problem, Doctor. My husband thinks he's a car.
  Doctor: Well, ask him to come in and I'll examine him.
  Woman: ....

3 **Doctor:** Now just stand by that window, Mrs Jackson, and put your tongue out.
  Patient: Why, are you going to examine my throat?
  Doctor: No, ...

4 **Patient:** Doctor, you must help me. I keep losing my memory.
  Doctor: I see, and when did this problem start?
  Patient: ....

5 **Patient:** Doctor, I get a terrible pain in my eye every time I drink tea.
  Doctor: ....

6 **Patient:** Doctor, I keep getting angry with everybody.
  Doctor: Pardon?
  Patient: ....

7 **Patient:** Doctor, I think I've got a problem with my eyesight.
  Man: ....

8 **Doctor:** Well, I'm afraid you've only got three minutes to live.
  Patient: Can't you do *anything* for me?
  Doctor: ....

---

a) I've told you once, you *idiot*!!
b) Well, I could boil you an egg.
c) Try taking the spoon out of the cup.
d) I know, I've been ill.
e) I think you have. This is the Post Office.
f) No, I can't do that. He's double parked!
g) Next, please!
h) When did *what* start?
i) It's because I don't like the people who live opposite.
j) No, I'm cleaning my glasses.

---

7 Now you're here

a Ask a British person:

How old do you have to be to:
ride a moped?
ride a motorbike?
drive a car?
go into a pub?
buy an alcoholic drink in a pub?
leave school?
get married?
go to prison?
vote in a general election?
smoke?

In Britain, do you have to:
carry an identity card?
do military service?
have a TV licence?
have a dog licence?
wear a crash helmet if your ride a moped?
wear a seat belt if you drive a car in town?
have insurance if you ride a moped or motorbike?
get married in church?

b Is it the same in your country?

What would you do?

1 If you found somebody's personal diary or a love letter, would you read it?

2 If somebody told you a very personal secret, would you tell anybody else that secret?

3 If a student, who never goes to classes, asked to copy all your notes before an exam, would you agree?

4 What would you do if somebody —a complete stranger—asked you for some money for a cup of tea or some food? Would you give him/her anything? (You've got plenty of money in your pocket.)

5 Somebody you know has bought something expensive to wear to a party. You don't like it at all. What would you say if he or she asked you for your opinion?

6 You're on your way to the back of a long cinema queue. What would you do if you saw somebody you knew in the queue? Would you go and join that person?

7 You're playing a tennis match and it's match point. If the other player hit a shot, and you weren't sure if it was in or out, would you call 'out'?

8 You're at a party. What would you do if your best friend's girlfriend or boyfriend started to flirt with you? Would you say anything to your friend?

9 You're babysitting for somebody, and you've got a boyfriend or girlfriend who lives a long way away. There's a phone in the house. What would you do if you wanted to ring him or her?

1 Which question?

Match the answers below with the questions on page 60.

Example: a – 7

a) 'Yes I would! I hate losing!'

b) 'It depends what it was. I'd probably just tell one other person.'

c) 'Yes, I'd look at the first page, to see if it was interesting!'

d) 'No, I wouldn't. I'd feel guilty if I did. It's like stealing, isn't it?'

e) 'Yes I would if I thought he/she was really poor.'

f) 'Yes, I'd stop and talk to him or her and then I'd stay.'

g) 'No, I wouldn't. If he/she's that lazy, why should I help?'

h) 'I'd tell the truth and say I didn't like it.'

i) 'I think I'd just make it clear I wasn't interested in him/her.'

2 How well do you know each other?

a Write down *your* answers to the questions on page 60.

b Sit with somebody you know quite well. Write down how you think the other person would answer the questions.

c Ask each other the questions. Were you right about each other's answers?

3 What's the problem?

Listen to four people discussing some of the questions on page 60. Write down the number of the question they're discussing.

a) ....

b) ....

c) ....

d) ....

4 What would you do with them?

What would you do or feel if somebody gave you the things below?

1 I'd smoke them.
I'd give them to my father because I don't smoke.
I'd say, 'No thanks, I don't smoke.'

2 ....

3 ....

4 ....

5 ....

6 ....

5 What would you choose?

Work in pairs. Take it in turns to ask and answer the questions. The student who answers has his/her book closed.

1 If you could spend one day anywhere in the world, where would you go?
2 If you could eat anything you liked this evening, what would you have?
3 If you could buy anything (a single object), what would you buy?
4 If you could be brilliant at one thing, what would you choose?
5 If you could change places with one person for one day, who would you choose?
6 If you could choose any job or profession, what would you be?
7 If you could meet anyone, alive or dead, who would you like to meet?

Grammar summary: page 86

1 Parts of the body

a How do you pronounce the words in the box? Label the picture using these words.

arm leg ear knee neck head back nose toes hand wrist ankle mouth throat tongue chest finger stomach shoulder foot/feet tooth/teeth eye

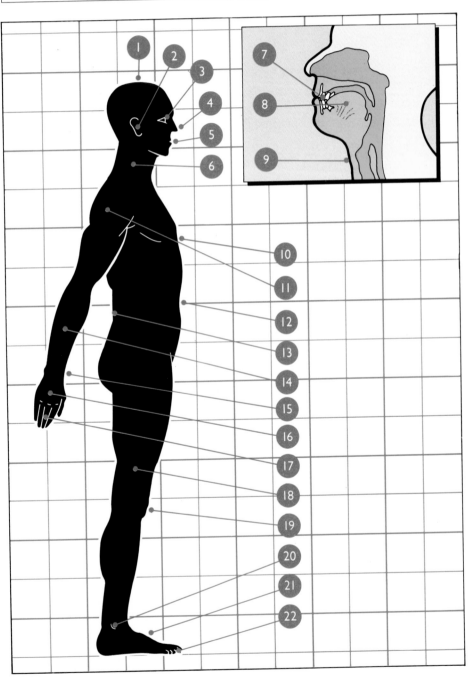

b Work in pairs. Student A points to a part of his/her body. Student B says what it is in English. Change roles.

2 Feeling ill

A You don't look very well. Are you feeling all right?
B No, I'm not really. I've got a sore throat and I think I've got a temperature.
A You'd better go to the doctor's. Do you want me to make an appointment for you?
B Yes please, could you?

a Practise this dialogue in pairs. Change roles.

b Now change the underlined words. Choose from the following:

I've got	a stomach ache.
	earache.
	a headache.
	a (bad) cold.
	a cough.
	flu.
	a pain in my back.

Why don't you	take an aspirin.
You should	go to bed.
You'd better	lie down.
	take some medicine.
	go to the doctor's.

c Change roles. This time choose from the following:

My	arm	hurts.	I feel	ill.
	leg			awful.
	shoulder			terrible
	back			dizzy.
				sick.

You'd better	take an aspirin.
You should	go to bed.
Why don't you	lie down.
	take some medicine.
	go to the doctor's.

3 What's the matter?

One student comes to the front of the class. The teacher writes down on a card (or whispers) what is wrong with him/her. The class ask the student, 'What's the matter?' The student *mimes* what is wrong and the class try to guess.

If the class guess correctly, they must give the student advice.

Example:
You should take an aspirin/go to bed.

4 🖭 At the doctor's

*Ah, come in Miss Strambini . . .
Now, tell me, what's wrong with you?
I've got a pain just here and a terrible headache which won't go away.
I see. How long have you felt like this?
For two days now.
Let me just feel it . . . does that hurt?
Ow! Yes, it does.
Yes, you've picked up a virus I'm afraid. There's a lot of it about at the moment. But I can give you a prescription for some antibiotics . . .
Now, take the medicine three times a day for a week and you'll soon feel better.
I'm sorry, I don't understand. What's this?
That's the prescription. Take it to the nearest chemist's and they'll give you the medicine.
Oh, I see. Thank you. Um . . . Do I have to pay you?
No, but you'll have to pay part of the cost of the medicine.*

WHAT'S THE MATTER?

B *Yes, I see. Well thank you very much doctor. Goodbye.*
A *Goodbye.*

a Practise the dialogue in pairs. Change roles.

b Now practise the conversation with other students, without looking in the book. Use your own ideas. Student B (the patient) can change his/her problem. Student A (the doctor) can change his/her advice.

5 What's the problem?

🖭 Listen to the conversation at the doctor's and fill in the missing information in the doctor's notes.

> Problems?
> How long for?
> His temperature?
> What's wrong?
> Prescription for?
> How many?
> How often?
> When/come back?

If you're ill in Britain

If you are from an EC (European Community) country or from one of these countries – Austria, Norway, Sweden, Yugoslavia (and some others), you can see a doctor, or ask him/her to visit you, or go to hospital, free.

If a doctor gives you a prescription, you get the medicine from a chemist's and pay for it there.

If you are not from one of the above countries you can still get emergency treatment free.

Summary of English in situations

- talking about parts of the body
- asking/saying what's the matter with you
- at the doctor's

1 ⊞ Sound right

a Listen to the words on the cassette. They all start with different sounds.

this   thin   top   day   sat   free

What are the six different sounds?

b Listen again and repeat the six words.

c Now listen to these words on the cassette. Tick the correct column according to which sound the word begins with.

d Listen again and repeat the words.

e Practise saying these:

thirty thousand trees
Think about these three things.
Thank your father and mother for everything.
I spent three months with them.

	[ð] this	[θ] thin	[t] top	[d] day	[s] sat	[f] free
1						
2						
3						
4						
5						
6						
7						
8						
9						
10						
11						

2 Listen to this

a ⊞ Listen to the voices on the cassette. How does the speaker feel in each situation? Choose from the words in the box.

embarrassed	worried	bored
interested	tired	scared
disappointed	excited	impatient
annoyed	unhappy	suspicious

b What do you think the situation is in each case?

3 Work on words

Match the words on the left with the words on the right.

Example: post office

1	**post**	a)	map
2	horror	b)	room
3	LP	c)	racket
4	summer	d)	call
5	passport	e)	box
6	love	f)	letter
7	credit	g)	sitter
8	tennis	h)	record
9	railway	i)	film
10	baby	j)	pot
11	travel	k)	door
12	front	l)	card
13	telephone	m)	holiday
14	underground	n)	**office**
15	tea	o)	station
16	changing	p)	crossing
17	traveller's	q)	control
18	international	r)	cheque
19	pedestrian	s)	licence
20	driving	t)	agent

4 Play games in English

What are they like?

a The class think of a person who everybody knows.

b Form two teams, A and B. Team A think of a sentence about that person using an adjective beginning with A.

c Team B then think of a sentence to describe the person but using an adjective beginning with B, etc.

Example:
Team A: *Fiona's an active girl.*
Team B: *Fiona's a brilliant girl.*
Team A: *Fiona's a careful girl.*

d If one team cannot think of an adjective in fifteen seconds and the other team can, they win a point.

e The game continues right through the alphabet to Z.

5 Read and think

a Read the following text.

There are 365 days in a year.

If you sleep 8 hours a day that comes to 122 days altogether.

This leaves 243 days left for work.

But there are 52 weekends a year. Each weekend is 2 days, which means you lose another 104 days a year for work.

This leaves 139 days for work.

But then you must remember that you spend at least one hour a day having breakfast and dinner. This comes to 15 days over a whole year.

This leaves 124 days for work.

But of course you can't work all that time – you need a holiday. Let's say you have three weeks' holiday.

Now you're left with 103 days for work.

But you don't work all day. Four free hours each evening takes up 61 days altogether.

This means you're left with only 42 days for work.

But then you have to remember that you get 2 days' holiday at Easter, 3 at Christmas, and 1 at the New Year. There are also 4 Bank Holidays.

Take those 10 days away and you're left with 32 days for work.

But then you have one and a half hour's lunch every day, and half an hour's coffee break. That comes to 30 days a year.

This means that, at the end of the year, you've only worked for two days.

It's not really surprising you don't get much work done!

b Why does there seem to be no time left for work? Compare your answers in groups.

6 Now you're here

Check with a British person to see if you know what these idioms and slang phrases mean.

1 Are you on the phone?
2 He nicked it!
3 She's only a kid.
4 Come off it.
5 I chatted her up.
6 I don't think much of this.
7 They get on well.
8 Can you lend me a quid?
9 Do you fancy going out?
10 I must be off.
11 I haven't a clue.
12 I couldn't help laughing.
13 Oh, by the way . . .
14 I'll see you home.
15 Do you feel like a coffee?
16 She's fed up with him.
17 He got the sack.
18 Have it your own way.
19 It rings a bell.
20 I don't get it.
21 Please yourself.
22 It's a rip-off.
23 I'm not made of money.
24 Take it easy.
25 Are you with me?
26 Get lost.
27 I'm completely broke.
28 It makes no odds.
29 It's up to you.
30 Can I have a word with you?

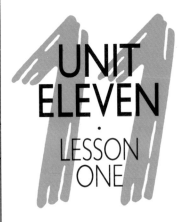

UNIT ELEVEN · LESSON ONE

GRAMMAR IN ACTION

Where do all the tourists go?

What are the most popular places for tourists in Britain? These are some of the top ten tourist attractions.

Madame Tussaud's Waxworks
(2.5 million visitors per year)

Madame Tussaud was a Frenchwoman who lived in Paris during the French Revolution. She was forced to make death masks of people who had been executed (many of them were her friends).

Her waxworks were opened in London in 1842. Many of her original models are still exhibited, but models of politicians, pop stars, and sporting personalities are changed regularly.

In the basement, the Chamber of Horrors can be visited — if you are brave enough!

Alton Towers
(2.4 million visitors per year)

Alton Towers was opened in 1978. It was recently voted 'Britain's most outstanding tourist attraction' and it has been described as Britain's Disneyland. Visitors are 'flown' on a Skyride over the gardens, soaked on the Grand Canyon Ride in Aqualand, and terrified by rides like the Corkscrew and the Black Hole.

The Roman Baths, Bath
(800,000 visitors per year)

The hot water springs in Bath were first discovered by the Romans in the first century A.D. The baths were built on the site and then used by the Romans for bathing and for the good of their health.

When the Romans left Britain, the baths were forgotten. They were not 'rediscovered' until 1878.

Nowadays, the Roman remains are visited by thousands of people. They also drink some of the famous hot water. Over a million litres a day of this water comes out of the ground at a constant temperature of 46.5°C.

The Tower of London
(2.1 million visitors per year)

The Tower was built by William the Conqueror in the eleventh century. It was lived in by English kings, until it was turned into a prison. Many famous prisoners, like Henry VIII's wife, Anne Boleyn, were executed there.

The Crown Jewels are kept in the Tower, where they are guarded by 'Beefeaters'.

It is said that if the famous ravens leave the Tower, England will be conquered. That is why the ravens' wings have been clipped.

I Make true sentences

1 Madame Tussaud 2 The Roman Baths 3 Anne Boleyn	are	executed in the Tower. built by William the Conqueror. forgotten and then rediscovered.
4 Madame Tussaud's waxworks	was	discovered by the Romans. forced to make death masks.
5 The Crown Jewels 6 Alton Towers	were	guarded by Beefeaters. flown on a Skyride over the gardens.
7 The Tower of London 8 The models	has been	described as Britain's Disneyland. opened in London in 1842.
9 Visitors to Alton Towers 10 The wings of the ravens 11 The hot water springs	have been	changed regularly. clipped.

2 Where are they?

🔊 Listen to the voices on the cassette and decide where the speakers are. Tick your answers. a = Madame Tussaud's, b = Alton Towers, c = The Tower of London, d = The Roman Baths.

	a	b	c	d
1				
2				
3				
4				
5				
6				
7				
8				

3 What's missing?

Work in pairs. Student A reads the instructions on this page. Student B reads the instructions on page 81.

Read the text about St Paul's Cathedral. There are ten gaps in it. Ask student B questions to find the missing information and answer his/her questions.

Example:
A *When was Old St Paul's started?*

Three churches were built on the site of St Paul's Cathedral before Old St Paul's was started in the (1 . . .) century. This huge Norman church took over (2 . . .) years to build. During the fifteenth and sixteenth centuries this great building was used not just as a church, but as a market for (3 . . .) and coal, and as a stable for horses. Old St Paul's was finally burnt down in the Great Fire of London in (4 . . .).

The architect Christopher Wren was asked by (5 . . .) to design a cathedral to replace it. This was begun in 1675. Wren supervised every stage of the work but he still found time to design over fifty other London churches. When the work was completed in (6 . . .) Wren was an old man. He was buried in 'his' cathedral when he died, aged 90, in the year 1723. Since then many other famous people have been buried in St Paul's, including Nelson and the (7 . . .).

During the Second World War the cathedral was very nearly destroyed by bombs. In 1981 (8 . . .) were married in St Paul's. Thousands of tourists visit the church every year. Most of them climb the (9 . . .) steps to the Whispering Gallery which runs round the inside of the dome. If you stand near the wall and you whisper something it can be heard on the opposite side of the dome, (10 . . .) metres away.

4 Quiz on Britain

a Form two teams. Team A answer question 1, Team B question 2, etc.

1 Who was born in Stratford-on-Avon?
2 Where is the FA Cup Final played?
3 Where are 'kilts' worn?
4 Which sport is played, more than any other, in Wales?
5 Where can the Changing of the Guard be seen?
6 Where is 'cockney' spoken?
7 Where were the Beatles born?
8 In which part of Britain can the Loch Ness Monster be 'seen'?
9 What is the sea between England and France called (by the English)?
10 Where can a 'Ploughman's' be eaten?
11 Where is most of Britain's oil obtained from?
12 Which three things are delivered to almost all British homes?
13 Which building is Big Ben situated next to?
14 England was invaded in 1066. Where did the invading army come from?
15 What sport is played at Wimbledon?

b Now think of your own questions like those above.

5 Where were they made?

a Make a list of all the things you are wearing and the things you've got in your bags/pockets, for example: jeans, shoes, sweater, watch, camera, comb.

b Work in pairs. Ask each other:
Where do you think | this . . . was made?
these . . . were made?

Example:
A *Where do you think these jeans were made?*
B *In Hong Kong.*
A *No, they weren't. They were made in Taiwan.*

Grammar summary: page 86

Rules of the house

① You must be on time for meals.

② You must come home before 11 o'clock.

③ You mustn't use the telephone without permission.

④ You mustn't have friends in your room.

⑤ You can't smoke in your room.

⑥ You can't have a bath without permission.

⑦ You are not allowed to play loud music in your room.

⑧ You are not allowed to take food or drink from the fridge without asking.

1 The rules of your house

Tick (✓) those rules above which are true in your family in Britain or in your family at home.

2 Can you or can't you?

Ask another student questions about the rules above:

Examples:
Can you come late for meals?   (Yes, I can./No, I can't.)
Do you have to come home before 11 o'clock?   (Yes, I do./No, I don't.)
Are you allowed to smoke in your room?   (Yes, I am./No, I'm not.)

Make notes of his/her answers. Then tell the rest of the class about the rules in his/her house.

3 Different families, different rules

Listen to these foreign students talking about their English families. Mark the things they are allowed to do with a tick (✓) and the things they are not allowed to do with a cross (x).

	come home late	smoke in his/her room	have a bath every day	have friends in his/her room
Michel				
Enrica				
Hans				
Yoko				

4 Role play

Work in pairs. Act out the conversations in these situations.

1

2

3

4

68

5 What are they doing wrong?

Many of the people in this picture are doing something wrong. Find the people and make sentences:

Examples:
You're not allowed to walk on the grass.
You mustn't drop litter.
You have to drive on the left.

6 What do the signs mean?

What do the following signs or symbols mean?

Example:
You're not allowed to / you mustn't smoke.

Summary of English in situations

- talking about rules and obligations

1 🔊 Sound right

a Listen to these phrases and sentences:

go to bed
a glass of milk
fish and chips
He's from France.
They sent us a card.
What do you want to eat?
What's the time? It's ten to ten.
It's a pound for half an hour.
I was in the bath at ten o'clock.
Would you like a cup of tea?

b Listen again and circle the unstressed words.

Example: (a) glass (of) milk

c Listen and repeat the phrases and sentences. Try to say the unstressed, 'weak' words as lightly and as quickly as you can.

2 Listen to this

🔊 Listen to this guided tour of part of the Tower of London. Mark the following statements true [√] or false [X].

1 Henry divorced his second wife. ☐
2 Three of Henry's wives were imprisoned in the Tower. ☐
3 Anne Boleyn was Henry VIII's third wife. ☐
4 Elizabeth I was Anne Boleyn's daughter. ☐
5 Anne was imprisoned in the Tower for 6 months. ☐
6 Her head was cut off with an axe. ☐

3 Work on words

Work in pairs. Student A looks at the instructions on this page. Student B looks at the instructions on page 81.

a Describe to student B what each thing (1–10) is used for. He/She will tell you what each thing is called. Fill in the words.

b Student B will describe what each of the things (11–20) is used for. Tell him/her what each thing is called.

Example:
A *What do you call a thing for measuring lines?*
B *A ruler.*

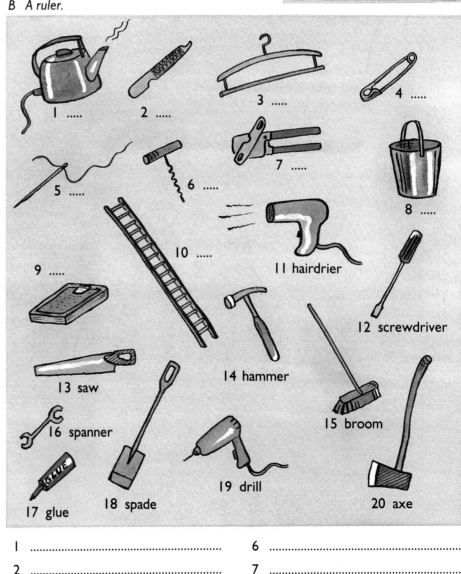

1 .....
2 .....
3 .....
4 .....
5 .....
6 .....
7 .....
8 .....
9 .....
10 .....
11 hairdrier
12 screwdriver
13 saw
14 hammer
15 broom
16 spanner
17 glue
18 spade
19 drill
20 axe

1		6 ....
2		7 ....
3		8 ....
4		9 ....
5		10 ....

4 Read and think

When's your birthday?

Follow these instructions carefully:

1 Write down the date of your birthday on a piece of paper. Example: June 11th 1963

2 Multiply the month of your birthday by one hundred. (June = 6. 6 × 100 = 600)

3 To this figure add the date (in days) of your birthday. (600 + 11 = 611)

4 Multiply this figure by two and then add eight.

5 Now multiply the number you have by five and then add four.

6 Multiply the number by ten and add four again.

7 Now add your present age to this figure.

8 Finally subtract four hundred and forty-four. What's the answer?

What the numbers mean:

The first number(s) is the month of your birthday.
The next number(s) is the day.
The last two numbers say how old you are.

5 Time to talk

Work it out

• Form groups of four or five students. Discuss your answers to the problem.

• Each group chooses a spokesperson who tells the rest of the class their answer.

The teacher decides which answer is best.

Three students stopped at a hotel for the night. The receptionist told them that there was only one room left, but they could have it for £30. The three students agreed to share the room.

RECEPTION

Late that evening the manager told the receptionist that the room cost only £25 a night – not £30. She sent a porter up to the room to tell the students that it only cost £25 and to give them £5 back.

The student who answered the door took the £5 from the porter but then gave him a tip of £2 so that she could divide the rest equally among the three of them.

This meant that each student paid £9 for the room, making a total of £27. The porter got £2. What happened to the £1?

6 Play games in English

Twenty Questions

a Student 1 writes down a word on a piece of paper. It can be:

an object, for example an iron
a person, for example a postman
a place, for example a park.

b The teacher checks the word and student 1 tells the class 'object', 'person' or 'place'.

c The class can ask a maximum of 20 questions to guess the word. Student 1 can only answer 'yes', 'no', or 'sometimes'.

Example:
Student 1 *'Object'*
Student 2 *Have you got one?*
Student 3 *Can you find it in the house?*
Student 4 *Is it bigger than me?*

d The person who correctly guesses the word chooses the next one. If no one guesses the word, student 1 wins and chooses a new 'student'.

e Now play the game in smaller groups.

7 Now you're here

Ask a British person what the following abbreviations are short for.

1 VAT	13 info.
2 p.m.	14 Mon.
3 a.m.	15 ctd
4 VHF	16 plc.
5 WC	17 prog.
6 DJ	18 tel.
7 ER	19 Dr
8 LP	20 hrs
9 B & B	21 doz.
10 e.g.	22 Xmas
11 VIP	23 dept
12 IRA	24 incl.

GRAMMAR IN ACTION

I Think back

Write short answers to these questions.

1 How did you come to Britain?

2 How long did the journey take?

3 Were you asked any questions at passport control? (Was your passport stamped?)

4 Were you stopped in Customs? (Was your luggage opened?)

5 What surprised you most when you first arrived in Britain?

6 How long have you been in Britain?

7 How much English did you understand when you first arrived?

8 In what ways has your English improved since you came?

9 Have you spoken to many British people?

10 Who have you spoken English to most?

11 What different things have you done in the evenings? (What have you most enjoyed doing?)

12 What's the weather been like?

13 What excursions/trips have you been on? (Which did you enjoy most?)

14 How much money have you spent? (What did you spend it on?)

15 Have you lost anything?

16 If you came back to Britain, where would you go? What would you do?

17 What do you think is the:
most old-fashioned | thing
most modern | about
worst | Britain?
best
strangest

18 What will you miss most?

19 What will you not miss?

20 When are you going to leave Britain?

21 Are you going to write to anybody when you get home?

22 In what ways have your opinions of Britain and the British people changed?

23 What has been your most:
embarrassing | experience?
unpleasant
enjoyable

2 Do you remember?

a Form two teams. In 5 minutes, each team writes at least ten questions about the Lesson 1 texts and stories in this book.

Example:
What did Jessica Wilson have for breakfast?
Why did the English film star in Hollywood want an old phone box?
Why was Mike Brain arrested?
What did Jimmy Denny say about Elvis Presley?

b Take it in turns to ask each other your questions. You get one point for a correct answer.

3 What's the difference?

a Form groups of four or five students. Discuss in groups the difference in meaning between these pairs of sentences.

b Compare your answers with those of other groups.

1 a) He's gone to Spain.

   b) He's been to Spain.

2 a) I'm speaking English.
   b) I speak English.

3 a) What do you do?
   b) What are you doing?

4 a) What did you do when the bomb exploded?
   b) What were you doing when the bomb exploded?

5 a) I was married for two years.
   b) I have been married for two years.

6 a) You mustn't go.
   b) You don't have to go.

7 a) What's he like?
   b) What does he like?

8 a) I'd like to dance.
   b) I like dancing.

9 a) It's a bottle of wine.
   b) It's a wine bottle.

10 a) Where are the boy's clothes?
   b) Where are the boys' clothes?

11 a) He wants to dance with me.
   b) He wants me to dance.

12 a) Have you got a paper?
   b) Have you got a piece of paper?

13 a) He worked hard.
   b) He hardly worked.

14 a) Is he still asleep?
   b) Is he asleep yet?

1   Saying goodbye

A *The taxi's waiting!*
B *OK, I'm coming.*
A *Are you sure you've got everything? Suitcase? Bags? Passport? Tickets?*
B *Yes. I think so.*
A *Good. Well, I hope you've had a good time.*
B *Yes, I've really enjoyed myself. Thank you very much for everything.*
A *That's all right. We've enjoyed having you. Give our regards to your parents.*
B *Yes, I will, don't worry. And thank you very much again.*
A *Don't forget to write to us.*
B *No, I won't. I promise.*
A *Have a good journey. Bye . . .*
B *Goodbye, and thank you.*

Practise the dialogue in pairs. Change roles.

2   What's the opposite?

a Form groups of four or five students. Discuss and then write down what the 'opposites' to B's answers are. There are many possible 'right' answers.

Example:

A *Would you like some more?*
B *Yes, please. / No thanks. I'm full.*

  1 A *Would you like to come too?*
      B *No thanks. I'm busy.*

  2 A *Is it all right if I smoke?*
      B *Yes, of course.*

  3 A *Are you being served?*
      B *Yes thanks.*

  4 A *Can I borrow £5, please?*
      B *Yes, here you are.*

  5 A *Do you like my new skirt?*
      B *Yes, it's very nice.*

  6 A *Anything else?*
      B *Yes, can I have two Mars Bars, please?*

  7 A *Excuse me. Can you tell me where the nearest Midland Bank is, please?*
      B *Yes, there's one in Prince Street.*

  8 A *Do they fit?*
      B *Yes, they're fine.*

  9 A *Can I speak to Mario, please?*
      B *Yes, just a moment.*

10 A *Can I take a message?*
      B *No, it's all right thanks.*

11 A *Are you doing anything special tonight?*
      B *No, nothing special.*

14 A *What's the matter?*
      B *Nothing, I'm fine.*

b Compare your answers with those of other groups.

3   What would you say?

Form two teams, A and B. Team A answers question 1, Team B question 2 and so on. If one team's answer isn't very good, the other team can try to answer it.

  1 A boy/girl asks you to dance. You don't want to dance with him/her.
  2 You're eating with your English family. You don't like the food. You're offered more.
  3 You ring a friend. Another person answers and tells you he's not in.
  4 You're in a clothes shop. You want to make sure that a pair of jeans fit you.
  5 You want to come home late but you haven't got a key.
  6 You're having a party. You want to invite a person you fancy but don't know very well.
  7 You're on a bus. When the conductor asks you for your fare you find you haven't got enough money.
  8 You answer the phone. The person at the other end asks to speak to David. You don't know anybody called David.
  9 You don't like cigarette smoke so you're sitting downstairs on a bus where it's non-smoking. The person next to you lights a cigarette.
10 Your landlady wants you to babysit. You've arranged to meet some friends.
11 Somebody offers you a lift home after a party. You think he's had too much to drink.
12 At the end of the meal with your English family you're still very hungry.
13 Somebody asks you a lot of questions but she speaks too fast for you to understand.
14 Somebody asks you how exactly to get from where you are now to the place where you're living.

4 What's missing?

a What do you think the other person is saying in these situations? / Write your answers.

1 A *I'm very sorry.*
  B ...

2 A *How would you like the money?*
  B ...

3 A *Would you like some more?*
  B ...

4 A *How do you do?*
  B ...

5 A *Thanks very much for everything.*
  B ...

6 A *Now, what's the problem?*
  B ...

7 A *Can I borrow your dictionary, please?*
  B ...

8 A *Have you got any means of identification?*
  B ...

9 A *Can I help you?*
  B ...

b Compare your answers in class.

1 🎧 Sound right

a Read each group of words aloud. What sound has each group got in common?

1 first   word   Thursday   learn   worse   bird
2 live   English   busy   biscuit   women   houses
3 fish   dictation   sugar   international   sure   shall
4 men   head   said   friend   many   says
5 you   blue   two   queue   fruit   through
6 fun   worry   enough   one   Monday   won
7 air   where   care   their   there   pear
8 daughter   walk   more   court   caught   thought

b Listen to the cassette and repeat each group of words.

c Think of other words that can be added to each group.

Example: 1 *her*

2 🎧 Listen to this

Listen to this half of a telephone conversation. You cannot hear what the person at the other end of the phone says.

a Listen all the way through for the general meaning.

b Form small groups. Listen again, discuss and then write down what you think the person at the other end said.

c Compare your answers with other groups'.

3 Play games in English

Noughts and crosses

a Form two teams, O and X.

b The teacher draws this table on the board:

SPELLING	ABBREVIATIONS	PLACES
WORDS	EXPRESSIONS	PREPOSITIONS
JOBS	PRONUNCIATIONS	OPPOSITES

c Team O chooses a category and the teacher asks only the first member of the team a question. If he/she answers correctly, the teacher writes an O in that space.

d If the answer is incorrect, the question is passed to team X. If they answer correctly then the teacher writes an X in the space.

e Team X have their own turn.

f The first team to get a straight line of Os or Xs in any direction is the winner.

4 Read and think

In groups, try to work out logical answers to these problems.

1 A woman staying in a hotel couldn't go to sleep. Suddenly she picked up the telephone and dialled the number of the room next door. A man answered 'Hallo?' in a sleepy voice. The woman just said, 'Oh, I'm sorry to disturb you. I've got the wrong number.' Then she rang off and almost immediately went to sleep. Why?

2 After a murder, the police interviewed three suspects. One man had been in a cafe, another on a plane. They both had witnesses. The third had been watching television, and could answer detailed questions about the programme which had been on at the time of the murder. Who did the police arrest, and why?

3 A man was walking alone along a jungle path, with a telephone box on his back. What did he use it for?

4 A man killed himself by jumping off a bridge into a river. When the police found him he had a broken neck. Why?

5 Work on words

a Form two teams, A and B.

b Each team looks at the list of verbs below and discuss what each word means.

c One member of team A demonstrates or mimes what the first word means, a member of team B does the same for the second word and so on. If one team make a mistake or don't know the meaning of a word, the other team can try.

1 stretch
2 sneeze
3 yawn
4 snore
5 hum
6 whisper
7 smile
8 laugh
9 hiccup
10 cough
11 lick
12 nod
13 wink
14 scream
15 lean
16 bow
17 kick
18 touch
19 drop

20 wave
21 hug
22 point
23 stroke
24 punch
25 whistle
26 kiss
27 shiver
28 clap
29 scratch
30 pat
31 rub
32 kneel
33 crawl
34 bite
35 throw
36 blow
37 stir
38 tear

6 How much have you noticed?

Form two teams, A and B. Take it in turn to answer these questions about Britain.

1 What is the speed limit:
   a) in towns?
   b) on motorways?
2 Who lives in 10 Downing Street at the moment?
3 What is the most common kind of English cheese?
4 How many TV channels are there in Britain? What are they called?
5 Name three of the four 'big' banks.
6 What number do you dial to call the police?
7 What colour is a £5 note?
8 Which political party is in power at the moment?
9 What do double yellow lines at the side of the road mean?
10 What is the name of the British flag? What colour is it?
11 Name five national daily newspapers.
12 What does a red L on a car mean?
13 Where are Lands End and John O'Groats?
14 What are the names of the two main London airports?
15 Name two main line London railway stations?
16 Name two bridges which cross the River Thames.
17 What is another name for the London underground?
18 What are the following animals?
   a) a spaniel
   b) a Jersey
   c) a Siamese
   d) a budgerigar
19 What do you expect to see at each of the following?
   a) Covent Garden
   b) the Old Vic
   c) the Tate
   d) the Victoria and Albert
20 What are the following short for?
   a) a pub
   b) a B and B

21 On which parts of your body would you wear the following?
   a) wellingtons
   b) a dinner jacket
   c) a bowler
   d) Y-fronts
22 How much do these cost?
   a) a second class stamp
   b) a first class stamp
   c) a stamp for a postcard to Europe
23 What are the following?
   a) a Penguin
   b) a Milky Way
   c) a Twix
   d) a Kitkat
24 What are each of the following?
   a) a council estate
   b) a semi-detached
   c) a bungalow
   d) a nursing home

25 What are the following?
   a) the RSPCA
   b) Dr Barnado's
   c) Oxfam
26 What are the following?
   a) A levels
   b) a degree
   c) GCSE
27 Who goes to each of the following?
   a) a primary school
   b) a comprehensive
   c) a public school
   d) a tech
   e) a kindergarten
   f) Oxbridge
28 What is the national anthem?
29 What are the following?
   a) hell's angels
   b) skins
   c) bikers
   d) yuppies
   e) rastas
30 What are the following products?
   a) Pal   e) Duracell
   b) Fairy Liquid   f) Weetabix
   c) Stork   g) Elastoplast
   d) Alpen   h) Kleenex

7 Time to talk

a Form groups. Write a short sketch which you are going to perform to the rest of the class.

The situation must take place in either:

a shop
a bank
a school
or
a plane.

You must include the following characters (and others):

a very deaf old man
a foreign student
a robber.

b Practise your sketch and then perform it in front of the class.

Unit 2 Lesson 1 Exercise 4
(page 13)

a Ask student A what he/she's going to do next week.

For each day, ask at least two questions.

Examples:
B *What are you going to do next week?*
A *I'm going to the cinema.*
B *What are you going to see/Who are you going with?*

b Look at your pictures. Student A is going to ask you what you are going to do next week. Answer the questions. Use you own ideas if necessary.

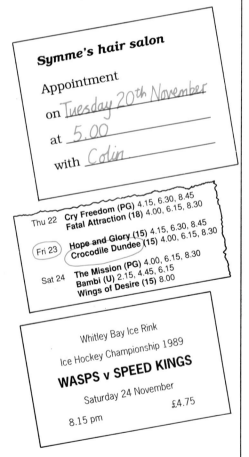

c Now write down what you are *really* going to do over the next few days. Answer A's questions. Then ask A what he/she's going to do.

Unit 3 Lesson 2 Exercise 4
(page 21)

You want to know where these places/buildings are:

1 the Town Hall
2 Barclays Bank
3 the post office
4 the police station
5 a Chinese take-away
6 the library

Find and mark them on your map with the information you get from Student A.

Take it in turns to ask and answer questions. (Student A starts.)

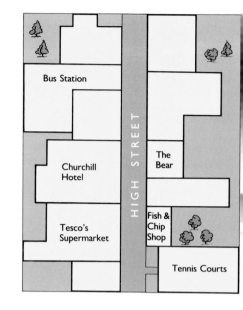

Unit 4 Lesson 1 Exercise 2
(page 25)

In pairs, ask each other questions about what the students in the first picture *were* doing.

Example:
A *What was the boy with glasses doing?*
B *I think he was reading a magazine.*

Who can remember the most?

Unit 4 Lesson 2 Exercise 5 (page 27)

Ask student A questions about these two people and fill in the missing information. Ask him/her to spell any difficult words.

Name: ....
Address: ....
Postcode: ....

Name: ....
Address: ....
Postcode: ....

Look at the information about these two people. Answer student A's questions about them:

Name: Stephanie Lawrence
Address: 61 Malmesbury Terrace
Durham
Postcode: DU15 2GJ

Name: Sean O'Malley
Address: 30 Newry Crescent
Ballymena
Northern Ireland
Postcode: BE11 9RI

Unit 4 Lesson 3 Exercise 5 (page 29)

Look at the pictures below. You have half of a story. Student A has the other half. Your pictures are *not* in the correct order. Describe your pictures to student A. Student A will describe his/her pictures to you. Try to put all twelve pictures in the correct order. Then tell the story between you. You must *not* look at Student A's pictures.

Unit 6 Lesson 1 Exercise 4 (page 37)

Read the information about these four people.

● James is older than Sarah.
● James isn't as old as Laura.
● Sarah isn't as tall as James.
● Sarah is taller than Daniel.
● James is heavier than Laura.
● Sarah isn't as heavy as Laura.

Ask each other questions to find out:

who's the oldest
who's the youngest
who's the tallest
who's the shortest
who's the heaviest
who's the lightest.

Example:
B *Is Daniel younger than Laura?*
A *No, he isn't. / Yes, he is. / I don't know.*

Unit 6 Lesson 2 Exercise 5 (page 39)

You are a sales assistant. You have only got three pairs of jeans left in your sale:

blue/size 27/£17.99
grey/size 28/£15.99
black/size 30/£19.45.

Talk to the customer and try to persuade him/her to buy a pair of jeans in your sale. Be very friendly.

Use phrases like these:

Can I help you?
What size are you?
They suit you.

Unit 8 Lesson 2 Exercise 5 (page 51)

You want to go to Brighton. Ask student A questions to get the information you need. He/She will ask you about a trip to Bath.

		To Bath	To Brighton
1	Cost of a day return ticket	£12.50	. . .
2	Time of the first coach you can catch	7.20	. . .
3	Time the coach arrives	11.20	. . .
4	Bay	6	. . .
5	Time of the last coach back	21.20	. . .

Unit 9 Lesson 2 Exercise 5 (page 57)

Read the information below.

Situation 1
Student A phones you to invite you to go out. You don't want to go out with him/her. Make excuses but be friendly.

Situation 2
Phone student A and invite him/her to go swimming at the beach with you. Try to persuade A to go with you.

Use phrases like:

Why don't you want to?
Oh, come on!
Are you sure?
Let's . . .
Shall we . . .
Why don't we . . .

Unit 9 Lesson 3 Exercise 2 (page 58)

Look at the picture below. Student A has a similar picture but with six differences. Describe your picture to Student A. Student A will describe his/her picture to you. Try to find the six differences.

Unit 11 Lesson 1 Exercise 3
(page 67)

Read the text about St Paul's Cathedral. There are ten gaps in it. Ask student A questions to find the missing information and answer his/her questions.

Example:
B *How many churches were built on the site of St Paul's Cathedral?*

(1 . . .) churches were built on the site of St Paul's Cathedral before Old St Paul's was started in the eleventh century. This huge Norman church took over two hundred years to build. During the (2 . . .) centuries this great building was used not just as a church, but as a market for vegetables and (3 . . .) and as a stable for horses. Old St Paul's was finally (4 . . .) in the Great Fire of London in 1666.

The architect Christopher Wren was asked by Charles II to design a cathedral to replace it. This was begun in (5 . . .). Wren supervised every stage of the work but he still found time to design over (6 . . .) other London churches. When the work was completed in 1710, Wren was an old man. He was buried in 'his' cathedral when he died, aged (7 . . .) in the year 1723. Since then many other famous people have been buried in St Paul's, including (8 . . .) and the Duke of Wellington.

During the (9 . . .) the cathedral was very nearly destroyed by German bombs. In (10 . . .) the Prince and Princess of Wales were married in St Paul's. Thousands of tourists visit the church every year. Most of them climb the 260 steps to the Whispering Gallery which runs round the inside of the dome. If you stand near the wall and you whisper something it can be heard on the opposite side of the dome, 32 metres away.

Unit 11 Lesson 3 Exercise 3 (page 70)

a Student A will ask you questions about what each of the things (1–10) below is called. Tell him/her the correct name.

Example:
A *What do you call a thing for measuring lines?*
B *A ruler.*

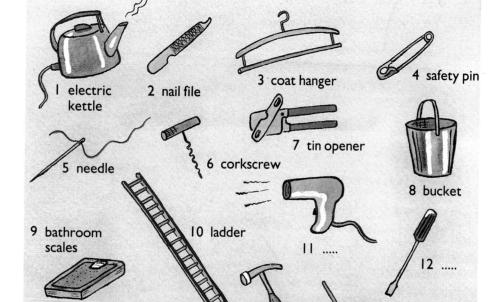

1 electric kettle
2 nail file
3 coat hanger
4 safety pin
5 needle
6 corkscrew
7 tin opener
8 bucket
9 bathroom scales
10 ladder
11 .....
12 .....
13 .....
14 .....
15 .....
16 .....
17 .....
18 .....
19 .....
20 .....

b Describe what each of the things (11–20) is used for. Student A will tell you what each thing is called. Fill in the words.

11	16 ....
12	17 ....
13	18 ....
14	19 ....
15	20 ....

Unit 1

to have got **(present tense)**

Affirmative

I	have (I've)	got ...
You	have (You've)	got ...
He	has (He's)	got ...
She	has (She's)	got ...
It	has (It's)	got ...
We	have (We've)	got ...
You	have (You've)	got ...
They	have (They've)	got ...

Negative

I haven't got ...
You haven't got ...
He hasn't got ...
She hasn't got ...
It hasn't got ...
We haven't got ...
You haven't got ...
They haven't got ...

Questions

Have I got ... ?
Have you got ... ?
Has he got ... ?
Has she got ... ?
Has it got ... ?
Have we got ... ?
Have you got ... ?
Have they got ... ?

The present simple tense

Affirmative

I	speak	
You	speak	
He	speaks	
She	speaks	English.
It	speaks	
We	speak	
You	speak	
They	speak	

Negative

I	do not	(don't)	
You	do not	(don't)	
He	does not	(doesn't)	speak
She	does not	(doesn't)	English.
It	does not	(doesn't)	
We	do not	(don't)	
You	do not	(don't)	
They	do not	(don't)	

Questions

Do	I	
Do	you	
Does	he	
Does	she	speak English?
Does	it	
Do	we	
Do	you	
Do	they	

Short answers

Yes, I do. / No, I don't.
Yes, you do. / No, you don't.
Yes, he does. / No, he doesn't.
Yes, she does. / No, she doesn't.
Yes, it does. / No, it doesn't.
Yes, we do. / No, we don't.
Yes, you do. / No, you don't.
Yes, they do. / No, they don't.

can **(present tense)**

Affirmative

I	can	
You	can	
He	can	
She	can	speak English.
It	can	
We	can	
You	can	
They	can	

Negative

I	cannot (can't)	
You	cannot (can't)	
He	cannot (can't)	
She	cannot (can't)	speak English.
It	cannot (can't)	
We	cannot (can't)	
You	cannot (can't)	
They	cannot (can't)	

Questions

Can I	
Can you	
Can he	
Can she	speak English?
Can it	
Can we	
Can you	
Can they	

Demonstratives

- For people / things which are here or near you, use *This* (singular) or *These* (plural).

- For people / things which are there or not near you, use *That* (singular) or *Those* (plural).

Unit 2

Present simple v present continuous

Use the present simple when you talk about what people do all the time, or again and again.

Example:
He works 48 hours a week.

Use the present continuous when you talk about what is happening *now*, at this moment.

Example:
I'm working. Go away!

Affirmative	
I am (I'm)	
You are (You're)	
He is (He's)	
She is (She's)	working.
It is (It's)	
We are (We're)	
You are (You're)	
They are (They're)	

Negative	
I'm not	
You aren't / You're not	
He isn't / He's not	
She isn't / She's not	working.
It isn't / It's not	
We aren't / We're not	
You aren't / You're not	
They aren't / They're not	

Questions	
Am I	
Are you	
Is he	
Is she	working?
Is it	
Are we	
Are you	
Are they	

The future tense: going to

Affirmative	
I am (I'm)	
You are (You're)	
He is (He's)	
She is (She's)	going to write.
It is (It's)	
We are (We're)	
You are (You're)	
They are (They're)	

Negative		
I am not	I'm not	
You are not	You aren't / You're not	
He is not	He isn't / He's not	
She is not	She isn't / She's not	going to write.
It is not	It isn't / It's not	
We are not	We aren't / We're not	
You are not	You aren't / You're not	
They are not	They aren't / They're not	

Questions	
Am I	
Are you	
Is he	
Is she	going to write?
Is it	
Are we	
Are you	
Are they	

some / any

- Positive sentences: *some*

  Example:
  They had some breakfast.

- Negative sentences: *any*

  Example:
  They didn't have any breakfast.

- Questions: *any*

  Example:
  Did they have any breakfast?

Countable nouns

- Positive sentences: *a lot of / a few*

  Examples:
  She meets a lot of people.
  A few guests are foreign.

- Negative sentences: *(not) many*

  Example:
  She doesn't get many tips.

- Questions: *many*

  Example:
  How many guests are there?

Uncountable nouns

- Positive sentences: *a lot of / a little*

  Examples:
  They leave a lot of rubbish.
  She speaks a little French.

- Negative sentences: *(not) much*

  Example:
  She doesn't earn much money.

- Questions: *much*

  Example:
  How much tea does she drink?

Unit 3

The past simple tense: regular verbs

Affirmative	
I	
You	
He	
She	walked.
It	
We	
You	
They	

Negative	
I You He She It We You They	didn't walk.

Questions		
Did	I you he she it we you they	walk?

Past simple tense: irregular verbs

Present	Past
be	was/were
begin	began
break	broke
bring	brought
buy	bought
come	came
cost	cost
do	did
eat	ate
find	found
forget	forgot
get	got
give	gave
go	went
have	had
hear	heard
know	knew
leave	left
lose	lost
make	made
meet	met
put	put
read	read

Present	Past
run	ran
say	said
see	saw
sell	sold
send	sent
shut	shut
sit	sat
sleep	slept
speak	spoke
take	took
tell	told
think	thought
write	wrote

There was / There were

Singular	Plural
There was . . .	There were . . .
There wasn't . . .	There weren't . . .
Was there . . . ?	Were there . . . ?

Infinitive of purpose

Use the infinitive with *to* when you give the reason for something.

Example:
He rang her to ask her to marry him.

Unit 4

The past continuous tense

Affirmative		
I	was	
You	were	
He	was	
She	was	eating.
It	was	
We	were	
You	were	
They	were	

Negative			
I	was not	(wasn't)	
You	were not	(weren't)	
He	was not	(wasn't)	
She	was not	(wasn't)	eating.
It	was not	(wasn't)	
We	were not	(weren't)	
You	were not	(weren't)	
They	were not	(weren't)	

Questions		
Was I Were you		
Was he Was she Was it		eating?
Were we Were you Were they		

Use the past continuous about something which was already happening when something else stopped or interrupted it (past simple).

Example:
They were driving on the motorway when
(past continuous)
the police arrested them.
(past simple)

Adverbs of manner

Adjective + *ly* = adverb	
quiet	+ *ly* = *quietly*
noisy	+ *ly* = *noisily*

Example:
The dog sat quietly.

Unit 5

The present perfect tense

Affirmative		
I You	have	
He She It	has	decided.
We You They	have	

Negative		
I You	have not (haven't)	
He She It	has not (hasn't)	decided.
We You They	have not (haven't)	

Questions		
Have	I you	
Has	he she it	decided?
Have	we you they	

Present perfect v past simple

Use the present perfect:

- about things which happened in the past but which still have an effect in the present.

  Example:
  I've lost my key.

- with *just, yet, already, never* and *ever*
- with *for* and *since*

Use the past simple:

- about things which happened in the past and are finished now, usually with words and phrases which indicated exactly when something happened.

  Example:
I lost my key	*yesterday.*
	last month.
	two days ago.

The present perfect tense: irregular verbs

Present	Past
be	been
begin	begun
break	broken
bring	brought
build	built
buy	bought
choose	chosen
come	come
cost	cost
do	done
eat	eaten
find	found
forget	forgotten
get	got
give	given
go	gone
have	had
hear	heard
hit	hit
know	known
leave	left
lose	lost
make	made
meet	met
put	put
read	read
run	run
say	said
see	seen
sell	sold
send	sent
shut	shut

Present	Past
sit	sat
sleep	slept
speak	spoken
take	taken
teach	taught
tell	told
think	thought
write	written

Unit 6

Comparatives of adjectives

- Add –*er* to short adjectives.

  Example: *short*
  Boys' names are usually shorter than girls' names.

- Put the word *more* before long adjectives.

  Example: *important*
  Your first name is more important than your middle name.

Irregular comparatives

good bad	better worse

Superlatives of adjectives

- Add –*est* to short adjectives.

  Example: *short*
  The shortest name.

- Put *the most* before long adjectives.

  Example: *popular*
  The most popular names.

Irregular superlatives

good bad	the best the worst

Unit 7

First conditional

Use *if* + the present simple to talk about things in the future which can happen or which are possible. Then use the future with *will* for the result. In other words, *If A happens, B will happen* or *B will happen if A happens.*

Examples:
If you go to England, you'll learn a lot of English.
You'll learn a lot of English if you go to England.

Unit 8

Relative pronouns who, which

Use *who* when you talk about people.

Example:
I can't stand people who look at themselves in shop windows.

Use *which* when you talk about things and animals.

Example:
I hate sitting on a seat which is still warm.

The gerund

The gerund is the verb + *ing.*

Use the gerund:

- after certain verbs, for example, *love, hate, enjoy, like, mind, go on, stop.*

  Example:
  I hate smiling for a photograph.

- after certain common expressions, for example:
  can't help / can't stand

  Example:
  People can't help telling me what's going to happen next.

- after prepositions:

  Examples:
  He wasn't excited about seeing me.
  I was blinking instead of smiling.

Unit 9

Use *so* or *not* after certain verbs, for example, *be afraid, expect, hope, suppose, think* when you do not want to repeat what somebody has just said or asked about.

Examples:
Do you think it'll rain?
Yes, I expect so. / No, I hope not.

Question tags

Use question tags when you are speaking to another person and you want to be sure he / she agrees with you. When you say something positive (+), make the question tag negative (−) with *not (n't).*

Examples:
     +   −
That's early, isn't it?
Shops close early, don't they?

When you say something negative, the question tag is positive.

Examples:
     −   +
You're not hungry then, are you?
You don't start school early, do you?

tell / want / ask somebody to do something

After the verbs *tell, want* and *ask* you can use an object followed by the infinitive with *to.*

Example:
They told me to go to bed.

Unit 10

The second conditional

Use *if* + the past simple (*If I found somebody's diary . . .*) to talk about things which are possible but not very probable. Then use *would* + a main verb for the result (*. . . I'd read it.*) In other words, *If A happened, B would happen.*

You can start the sentence with *B would happen* and follow it with *if A happened.* The meaning of the sentence is the same.

Example:
They'd use the phone if they were babysitters.
   or
If they were babysitters, they'd use the phone.

somebody / anybody / something / anything, etc.

A number of words begin with *some* or *any.* Use them like this:

somebody / anybody
someone / anyone } about people

something / anything   about things
somewhere / anywhere   about places

Use these words in the same way as *some* and *any.* In positive sentences, use *somebody, someone, something* or *somewhere.*

Example:
Someone you know has bought something expensive to wear for a party.

In negative sentences and in questions use *anybody, anyone, anything* or *anywhere.*

Example:
I didn't know anybody at the party.
Would you give him anything?

Unit 11

The passive

Form the passive with the verb *to be* + the past participle.

Present simple passive:

Examples:
The Tower of London is visited by millions of people.
The Crown Jewels are kept in the Tower.

Past simple passive:

Example:
The ravens' wings have been clipped.

Unit 1

surname
spell (v)
language
Dutch
a bit of
of course
worry (v)
neither
programming
computer
really?

Unit 2

need (v)
temporary
seaside town
bed and breakfast
guest house
compared to
awake
cereals
toast
fried egg
bacon
sausage
greasy
plate
hoover
complain
noise
guest
change (v)
sheet
make a bed
tidy (v a)
cap
toothpaste
make a mess
rubbish
everywhere
egg yolk
left (remaining)
foreigner
practise
earn
tip (n)

Unit 3

for sale
(tele) phone box
decide
get rid of
old fashiond
aluminium
agree
keep

> This list contains the new, active vocabulary introduced in each unit.
> The words are listed in the order in which they appear in the text.

reason
tropical
aquarium
racing pigeon
film star
homesick
remind
couple
fed up
endless
in peace
changing room
one-way glass
wedding present
knock (v)
marry
run out

Unit 4

funeral
afterwards
comment
scarf
judge (n)
fine (v)
arrest (v)
hitch (v)
protest (v)
court
get a lift
wear
blond
wig
heel
mini-skirt
German Shepherd
guard (v)
luxury
break in (v)
burglar
set off
alarm
unfortunately
quietly
calmly
cash (n)
jewellery
worth (a)
safe (n)
proudly
empty
enter
immediately
tear (tore)

Unit 5

point of view
foreign
strange
notice (v)
reply (n)
receive
so far
touch (v)
hug (v)
cheek
stroke (v)
pat (v)
explain
yours faithfully
pedestrian
   crossing
single
car horn
surprising
darling
stranger
love (greeting)
shop assistant

Unit 6

common
opposite
translate
Ms
instead of
choose
according to
survey
embarrassing
original

Unit 7

fly (v)
reach (v)
inventor
amazing
invention
ever
world war
historian
sink (v)
designer
lifetime

editor
magazine
market
chairman
learn
act (v)
movies
producer
succeed
business
truck
last (v)
prime minister

Unit 8

pet hate
mind (v)
flash (n)
blink (v)
can't stand
can't help
happen
annoy
greedy
past (= by)
piece
toast
butter
seat
teethmark

Unit 9

suppose
factory
office
close (v)
midnight
country
almost
I'm afraid so

Unit 10

diary
secret (n)
copy (v)
queue (n)
join
match point

hit (v)
shot
call (v)
flirt (v)
babysit

Unit 11

top (ten)
attraction
wax works
visitor
during
the French
   Revolution
force (v)
death mask
execute
original
exhibit (v)
politician
pop star
personalities
basement
Chamber of
   Horrors
brave
enough
recently
vote (v)
outstanding
describe
soak (v)
ride
terrified
conqueror
century
turn into
prison
crown jewels
Beefeater
raven
conquer
clip
spring (n)
discover
AD
site
health
until
remains
ground
daily
C = centigrade/
   Celsius

Unit 12

course
journey
passport control
stamp (v)
customs
luggage
improve
trip (n)
spend
lose (lost)
worst
miss (v)
embarrasing
experience
unpleasant
enjoyable

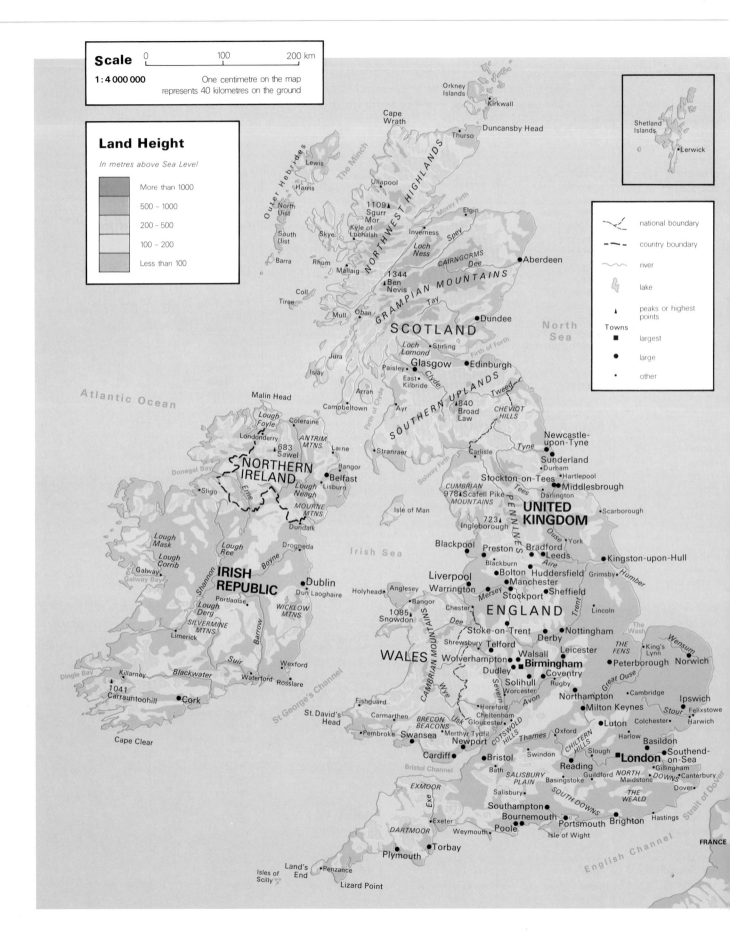

Scale

0   100   200 km

1 : 4 000 000   One centimetre on the map
                     represents 40 kilometres on the ground

Land Height

In metres above Sea Level

More than 1000
500 – 1000
200 – 500
100 – 200
Less than 100

national boundary
country boundary
river
lake
peaks or highest points

Towns
largest
large
other